*"I do not think that the pioneer women have ever had
the praises and credit that is due them for
their part in making this great northwestern
country what it is."*

Eliza Spalding Warren, 1916

MORE THAN PETTICOATS SERIES

More Than
PETTICOATS

REMARKABLE
IDAHO WOMEN

L. E. Bragg

TWODOT

Guilford, Connecticut

An imprint of the Globe Pequot Press

A · TWODOT · BOOK

Cover photo courtesy of University of Idaho Library Special Collections.

Library of Congress Cataloging-in-Publication Data

Bragg, L. E. (Lynn E.), 1956-
   More than petticoats: remarkable Idaho women/L. E. Bragg.—1st ed.
      p. cm. — (More than petticoats series)
   Includes bibliographical references and index.
   ISBN 0-7627-1123-X
      1. Women—Idaho—Biography. 2. Women—Idaho—History. I.
   Title. II Series.

CT3260 .B746 2001
920.72'09796—dc21

                                                    2001023469

CONTENTS

ACKNOWLEDGMENTS

$\mathcal{J}$ dedicate this book to a truly remarkable Idaho lady, Dede Wilhelm. Dede was my eyes, ears, and legs in Idaho, and I could not have completed the stories of these women without her. I am proud to call her a relative.

A world of thanks also goes to Troy Reeves, Oral Historian for the Idaho State Historical Society, for his assistance in person and via e-mail and the postal service.

Special thanks to Terry Abraham, Head of Special Collections and Archives for the University of Idaho Library; Mary Lee Lien, Director of the Bannock County Historical Society and Museum; Father Thomas Connolly, S.J., of the Sacred Heart Mission in DeSmet, Idaho; Kathy Hodges of the Idaho State Historical Society; Robert Matuozzi of Washington State University Library Special Collections; Nancy Gale Compau of the Spokane Public Library's Northwest Room; Karen De Seve of the Cheney Cowles Museum; the librarians who maintain the wonderful Northwest collection at the Seattle Public Library; Barbara (Ware) Featherstone and Nancy (Newton) Axell, for their suggestions; Marcia Glenn, whose children were godchildren to Margaret Cobb Ailshie; and Darla Moore, descendant of Porivo/Sacajawea.

Also, to the editor of my first "More than Petticoats" book, Megan Hiller, I thank you for bringing me into the series and guiding me through the Washington book. To Charlene Patterson, editor of the Idaho book, thank you for your work in bringing *More Than Petticoats: Remarkable Idaho Women* to fruition.

As always, special thanks to my mom, Polly Bragg, for her continuing support, encouragement, and editing skills, even when facing her own life challenges.

ꞘNTRODUCTION

Ꞙrom Sacajawea to silent films, Idaho women have played many unique roles in the development of the state. As we approach the two-hundredth anniversary of the Lewis and Clark Expedition, interest in Sacajawea and her part in the history of the Pacific Northwest is intensifying. The actions of the women profiled in this book, including Sacajawea and filmmaker Nell Shipman, continue to affect the state of Idaho by attracting tourists eager to see the historical sites impacted so many years ago by these women.

The real characters within these pages were all born before 1900. All made a profound impact on Idaho, from accompanying explorers to publishing Idaho's stories, past and present. Some people could argue that the actions of a few of these women proved detrimental to their own race: Sacajawea and Jane Silcott guided white men into the Northwest and showed them where gold was to be found. The actions of both, and of Louise Siuwheem in assisting the priests, certainly changed the destiny of their tribes. These actions, however, are part of Idaho's history, and these native women played pivotal roles in that history.

The women within these pages settled the Northwest, contributed to Idaho's economic development, fought for women's rights, reported the news, discovered the past, and showcased the beautiful Gem State. A history of Idaho unfolds through the stories of these courageous pioneer and native women. Their stories are told in the hope that we will remember and revere their legacies.

SACAJAWEA

1788–1812 OR 1884

Wadze-wipe, Lost Woman of the Lemhi Shoshone

*A*s the men of the expedition dragged their boats up the Beaverhead River, the seventeen-year-old Shoshone girl, her baby secure in a cradleboard strapped to her back, walked along the bank of the river with her French-Canadian husband and the red-haired Captain Clark. The trio had gone but a mile when the girl began to leap and dance in a showing of extreme joy. She turned to Captain Clark and gestured toward a group of Indians approaching on horseback. In her excitement the young girl sucked the fingers of her hand as a sign that the riders were Shoshone, her native tribe. It was seven o'clock in the morning of Saturday, August 17, 1805, when Sacajawea was reunited with her tribe.

The group continued toward the Shoshone camp, where a crowd of Shoshone people awaited their arrival. A young woman burst through the group and warmly embraced the Shoshone girl arriving with the white men. The tender affection between these two young Shoshone women upon their reunion was a scene that touched the hearts of the travel-weary explorers.

Statue honoring Sacajawea in Portland, Oregon

The women had been childhood friends, born and raised in what is now Idaho's Lemhi Valley. They had shared the same fate when, as girls, both had been taken prisoner by a raiding tribe of Hidatsa, or Minnetaree.

While Sacajawea was deep in conversation with friends she had thought she would never see again, Captain Clark proceeded on to meet with Captain Lewis and the Shoshone chief Cameahwait. The white men entered a circular tent made of willows, where the chief was seated on a white robe. Cameahwait's hair had been cut short to signify that he was in mourning for deceased relatives. All in the party removed their moccasins and commenced smoking pipes to open the meeting between them. The opening ceremony done, Sacajawea was summoned, as her interpreting services were needed.

She entered the shelter with eyes cast downward in a show of respect, sat down, and started to interpret for the men when a shock of recognition swept over her. Jumping to her feet, she ran to the chief, embraced him, and threw her blanket over him while tears of joy streamed down her cheeks. Chief Cameahwait was deeply moved as well, though he retained the composure expected of one in his position.

Sacajawea and Chief Cameahwait, brother and sister, were reunited. The siblings exchanged conversation, and Sacajawea presented her brother with a lump of sugar, which he later declared was the best thing he had ever tasted. Then, remembering her duty, Sacajawea took her seat and tried to resume interpreting for the council, but, overpowered by her emotions, she erupted into tears frequently throughout the meeting.

When the council had concluded, Sacajawea learned that most of the members of her family had perished. All that remained alive were Cameahwait, another brother who was not then among the tribe, and one young son of her oldest sister. In Shoshone fashion Sacajawea adopted her sister's young son, but he was left in the care of Cameahwait when the expedition left the camp.

Sacajawea, a member of the Lemhi Shoshone tribe, commonly referred to as the Snake[1] Nation in the days of the Lewis and Clark Expedition, was born in Idaho's Lemhi Valley around 1788. Though the Lemhi country was home to this tribe of Northern Shoshone, they traveled widely, following their food sources—digging roots and gathering berries in the mountains and valleys and hunting buffalo on the Plains.

On one such buffalo hunt, the tribe was camped at the Three Forks of the Missouri River in what is now Montana when they were attacked by their mortal enemies, the Hidatsa, also known as the Minnetaree or Gros Ventre. Many Shoshone were killed in the raid while younger children were taken captive. Twelve-year-old Sacajawea and two of her close friends were among those captured to be taken down the Missouri River to the Hidatsa villages of earthen lodges on the Knife River (in what is now North Dakota) to be enslaved, traded, or gambled away.

One of Sacajawea's friends was able to escape her captors and return to the Shoshone. According to the Shoshone the escapee was able to get away by leaping through a stream and was subsequently named *Pop-pank*, meaning "Jumping Fish." The other friend attempted to make her escape by sliding into the water like an otter, earning the name *Ponzo-bert*, or "Otter Woman." Sacajawea, who had been captured midstream while trying to escape from the Hidatsa, was called *Wadze-wipe*[2], or "Lost Woman," by her people since nothing was known of her ultimate fate. The Hidatsa referred to their captives as *Poo-ey neeve*, or "Maidens of the Grass People."

---

[1] The Shoshone called themselves "the people of the grass," but when attempting to convey their name in sign language, the sign for waving grass was interpreted as "snake." The Snake River is named after the misnomer for this tribe.

[2] By some accounts the name Wadze-wipe was given to Sacajawea in later life by the Comanche tribe.

Otter Woman and Sacajawea lived among the Hidatsa and their neighboring tribe, the Mandan, for the next five years of their young lives. During their captivity the girls were acquired, either through purchase or gambling, by a French Canadian named Toussaint Charbonneau, who lived among the tribes. While living in these Hidatsa-Mandan villages with Charbonneau and Otter Woman, the teenaged Sacajawea, now pregnant with her first child, was to have an encounter that would profoundly affect history.

In 1803 President Thomas Jefferson formed an expedition to explore the newly acquired Louisiana Purchase Territory that extended to Montana's western border. The expedition was to establish an American presence in the Northwest and explore a route of travel by water between the Atlantic and Pacific Oceans. Captain Meriwether Lewis, Jefferson's personal secretary, was named to lead the expedition. He, in turn, hired his army friend, Captain William Clark, to share the responsibility for leading the Corps of Discovery. The men of the Corps of Discovery left their quarters near St. Louis on May 14, 1804, and began their journey up the Missouri River.

By late October 1804 they had reached the Mandan villages of present-day North Dakota. Fort Mandan was established to provide winter quarters for the Corps as they prepared for their long journey toward the Pacific Coast. During the winter camp Toussaint Charbonneau approached the expedition leaders and asked to be hired as an interpreter. Charbonneau's reputation was less than stellar, but he knew Hidatsa and sign language; and when the captains learned that his wives were Shoshone, they quickly appreciated the value of having a Shoshone "interpretress" with them. The Shoshone, whom Lewis and Clark referred to as the Snake Nation, were reputed to be rich in horse stock, and the captains planned to obtain horses from them in order to cross the Rocky Mountains.

Charbonneau was hired as an interpreter with the understanding that he would bring with him one of his Shoshone wives. Sacajawea was chosen to accompany Charbonneau.

While at Fort Mandan awaiting departure, Sacajawea gave birth on February 11, 1805, to her son, Jean Baptiste Charbonneau. During the difficult birth of Baptiste, the young mother was attended by members of the expedition including Captain Lewis. Lewis wrote in his journal, "About five o'clock this evening one of the wives of Charbono was delivered of a fine boy. It is worthy of remark that this was the first child which this woman had born, and as is common in such cases her labor was tedious and the pain violent."

Lewis and Jessaume, another interpreter, administered the powdered rattle of a rattlesnake to the young mother, and within ten minutes she gave birth. As was common among the Shoshone, Sacajawea called her first born Pomp, meaning "head," or "leader."

When spring arrived, the expedition prepared to set out through the unexplored wilderness. Captain Lewis recorded the new additions to the expedition: "Our party now consists of the following individuals: interpreters George Drewyer and Taussant Charbono; also a black man of the name of York, servant to Captain Clark, and an Indian woman, wife to Charbono, with a young child."

On April 7, 1805, they began the trip up the Missouri River in six canoes and two large riverboats, called pirogues. The expedition would follow the Missouri to the Rocky Mountains in Montana, where they planned to acquire horses to transport them over the mountains.

Lewis and Clark were expected to study the geology, vegetation, and animal life found along the route and to report their findings to Jefferson. They were also to make contact with and document the various tribes they encountered, while promoting peaceful relations with them. Accordingly, both men kept detailed journals, recording events and findings on a daily basis, and they encouraged their men to do the same.

In order to better observe the environment, the captains made a practice of walking along the riverbanks while the boats proceeded upriver. Captain Clark, Charbonneau, and Sacajawea spent most days walking along the shore together. Clark developed a strong bond with Sacajawea and her baby, whom he referred to as Janey and Pomp.

Sacajawea's knowledge and skill in finding and preparing food for the party became evident early in the journey. Lewis records that the girl located and dug up hordes of wild artichokes that had been stored in the ground by mice. She introduced the group to many native roots and berries, bringing variety to their diet of wild game.

A near crisis occurred one day when the party was hit by a sudden windstorm while Charbonneau was steering one of the larger boats, laden with supplies. The vessel nearly capsized, and supplies spilled overboard. While her husband dropped the tiller and wailed in panic, Sacajawea calmly scooped up as many articles as she could from the river. Without her efforts clothing, navigational equipment, and other necessities would have been lost. According to Lewis,

> The loss we sustained was not so great as we had at first apprehended. . . . The Indian woman, to whom I ascribe equal fortitude and resolution with any person on board at the time of the accident, caught and preserved most of the light articles which were washed overboard.

A week later Lewis and Clark honored Sacajawea's valor by naming a river after her. "This stream we called Sah-ca-ger-we-ah or Bird Woman's River after our interpreter, the Snake woman," wrote Lewis.

Beyond the obvious natural hazards the Corps faced, insects, snakes, and dirty food and water threatened their health on a daily basis. By June Sacajawea was stricken with a high fever and excruciating stomach pains. The captains worried about Sacajawea, the baby in her arms, and the effect losing her would have on the future of the entire expedition. Lewis noted that she was the party's "only dependence for a friendly negotiation with the Snake Indians, on whom we depend for horses to assist us in our portage from the Missouri to the Columbia River."

Lewis applied herbal folk remedies to the sick woman, and with one relapse, Sacajawea recovered within two weeks.

When the expedition approached the Great Falls in present-day Montana, it became necessary to drag their canoes around a series of five waterfalls. This journey of 18 miles was to take them ten days. During the overland excursion Captain Clark, Charbonneau, and Sacajawea, with Jean Baptiste, were caught by a flash flood through a creek bed. The trio scrambled to higher ground, Clark pushing Sacajawea, with baby in her arms, up the hill, while Charbonneau, "much scared and nearly without motion," made vain attempts to assist. Wet to their waists, the group eventually reached the hilltop, where they found Clark's servant, York, searching desperately for them. They were safe, but little Baptiste's cradleboard and all of his clothing had been swept away.

The journals often refer to Charbonneau as cowardly and panic-stricken, while commending Sacajawea for her resourcefulness, calm acts of courage, and uncomplaining nature. Lewis's journal refers to an incident when Clark found Charbonneau striking his wife and reprimanded the interpreter severely, ordering him never to hit Sacajawea again. The beating may have been the result of Charbonneau's offering Sacajawea to the men of the expedition, as he was later known to do with other Indian wives. A recorded incident describes Charbonneau, then in his eighties, offering his newly acquired fourteen-year-old Indian wife to the men of his camp. Had this been the case with Sacajawea, as a Shoshone woman she would have found this unacceptable and would have endured a beating rather than submit to such a degradation.

In late July the Corps was in western Montana. Sacajawea began to recognize the country and assure the explorers that they were on the right trail. The captains named a creek she recognized White Earth Creek when she told them that the creek banks were a source of the white earth the Shoshone used to make white paint.

Curiously, the expedition had not encountered any Indians in this territory, though Sacajawea frequently pointed out signs of prior Indian habitation. The leaders began to doubt they would find the Shoshone, from whom they desperately needed horses.

By the time the expedition had reached the Three Forks of the Missouri, they were tired, sick, and losing faith in ever encountering a tribe with horses. Sacajawea brought hope to the men, assuring them that they were near the Shoshone. She explained to them that their present camp was on the very site where her tribe had been camped five years before when the Hidatsa attacked them. She demonstrated her capture and showed them the shallow place where she had been trying to cross the river when she was taken prisoner. She knew the summer camp of the Shoshone was near, and she was clearly familiar with the land and rivers.

Lewis and a small party of men had the first encounters with the Shoshone, all of whom fled Lewis's advances. He was finally able to overtake two women and a child and convince them, with presents and signs of friendship, to take him to their camp. Captain Lewis met with the head chief, Cameahwait, and further gained the trust of the Shoshone by supplying them with deer meat. Some of the subchiefs were still suspicious of the white men, and it was up to Lewis to convince them that Captain Clark's party, pushing their boats up the Beaverhead River, would be peaceful arrivals. He explained that they had a Shoshone woman and child with them. Lewis and some of the Shoshone set out together to ensure a friendly encounter with Captain Clark and the main party.

John Rees, who lived among the Lemhi Shoshone for fifteen years beginning in 1877, provided one account of Sacajawea's naming during this encounter. On the occasion of Sacajawea's reunion with her people, when all were dancing with joy, the Shoshone began making their signs for boat and calling her Sacajawea, or "one who travels with the boat that is pulled." The Shoshone sign for boat, made with a rowing motion of the arms, was misinterpreted by Charbonneau, who told Clark that the name meant "bird woman."

One of the great mysteries of Sacajawea's life is the source and spelling of her name. Traditionally, an Indian was given many names throughout his or her life, and without a written language, all Indian names are subject to interpretation when transcribed into English. Lewis and Clark used very innovative spelling in their journals, spelling both Sacajawea's and Charbonneau's names differently nearly every time they wrote them, though they usually did use a *g* as the middle consonant in her name.

It is generally accepted that *Sacagawea* or *Sakakawea* are Hidatsa words meaning "bird woman," whereas *Sacajawea* is of Shoshone origin and means "boat pusher." Although our government has chosen the Hidatsa version, *Sacagawea*, for their newly minted dollar coin, this author prefers to use Idaho's Lemhi Shoshone version, *Sacajawea*.

The Corps spent a week with the Shoshone, making saddles and preparing for their passage through the mountains. Goods that could not be packed on horseback were cached, or hidden, for the return trip. Through Sacajawea Lewis and Clark successfully traded for horses to take them to the Columbia River, and they obtained a guide to show them the route. Sacajawea also informed the leaders of her brother's intention to leave on a buffalo hunt before the expedition was fully equipped and safely underway. Cameahwait was then persuaded to delay his Plains buffalo hunt.

One problem they encountered during their stay with the tribe occurred when an older man claimed that Sacajawea had been betrothed to him by her father prior to her capture. The man already had two wives, and since Sacajawea had a child by another man, her betrothed was easily dissuaded.

Though Sacajawea had been overjoyed during the reunion with her family and tribe, she showed little emotion when leaving them as the expedition continued to the coast. She had made an agreement, through her husband, to stay with the expedition all the way to the Pacific and back. To have remained with her people rather than continue on, as promised, would have been dishonorable. Captain Lewis wrote of her tremendous ability to accept her lot in life and be happy with whatever fate befell her.

Guided by an old Shoshone man, the Corps continued west over Nez Perce trails. Upon reaching the Nez Perce tribe, they branded their horses, left them with the Nez Perce chief Twisted Hair, and continued on by canoe until they reached the Columbia River, which ultimately took them to their final destination.

Sacajawea's and Pomp's very presence with the explorers conveyed their message of being a peaceful expedition, as Clark recorded:

The wife of Shabono our interpreter we find reconciles all the Indians, as to our friendly intentions a woman with a party of men is a token of peace . . . the sight

of this Indian woman . . . confirmed those people of
our friendly intentions, as no woman ever accompanies
a war party of Indians in this quarter.

Rather than attack the party, the Indians they encountered
sought to communicate with the leaders of the expedition out of
curiosity. During these communications Sacajawea was often the
mediator as well as the interpreter. The interpreting was a
complicated and time-consuming process, as in the expedition's
dealings with the Chopunnish (Nez Perce) tribe, who had with
them a captive Shoshone boy. William Clark described the interpreting process:

It was not without difficulty, nor until after nearly half
the day was spent, that we were able to convey all this
information to the Chopunnish, much of which might
have been lost or distorted in its circuitous route
through a variety of languages; for in the first place we
spoke in English to one of our men, who translated it
into French to Chaboneau; he interpreted it to his wife
in the Minnetaree language, and she then put it into
Shoshonee, and the young Shoshonee prisoner
explained it to the Chopunnish in their own dialect.

In November 1805 the Corps of Discovery reached the
Pacific Ocean. By Captain Clark's calculations they were now
4,132 miles and 554 days from their original point of departure.
The men of the expedition built their winter quarters at Fort
Clatsop, where they remained until March 23, 1806. While at
Fort Clatsop, repairs were made to clothing and equipment, and
trading was conducted with local tribes. Sacajawea sacrificed her
own precious blue-beaded belt so that Captain Clark could trade

with a local Indian for a fur robe that he desired.

During their winter layover on the Pacific, a whale was discovered washed up on the beach. Lewis and Clark planned to send out a party to retrieve oil and blubber from the giant mammal. Hearing of this great oddity, Sacajawea begged to go with the men to see "the large fish." Although they had been camped only a few miles inland from the Pacific for two months, this was the first time Sacajawea would see the ocean.

In spring of 1806 the Lewis and Clark Expedition began their return journey. When they passed through Sacajawea's homeland, there was no sign of her people, except for a campfire and two horses. She and Charbonneau continued on with the expedition until they returned to the Mandan villages. On Saturday, August 17, 1806, Charbonneau, Sacajawea, and little Jean Baptiste terminated their services with the Corps of Discovery. Clark recorded their departure:

> Settled with Touisant Chabono for his services as an interpreter the price of a horse and lodge purchased of him for public service in all amounting to $500.33⅓ cents . . . we also took our leave of T. Chabono, his Snake Indian wife and their son child who had accompanied us on our route to the Pacific Ocean in the capacity of interpreter and interpretess. I offered to take his little son a beautiful promising child who is 19 months old to which they both himself and wife were willing provided the child had been weaned. They observed that in one year the boy would be sufficiently old to leave his mother and he would then take him to me if I would be so friendly as to raise the child for him in such a manner as I thought proper, to which I agreed.

In a letter to Charbonneau written a few weeks later, Clark reiterated his interest in raising Jean Baptiste and commended Sacajawea, or Janey, for her invaluable services, expressing regret that he had not been able to properly compensate her.

William Clark made good on his offer to educate Jean Baptiste, who even studied in Europe for six years as a young adult.

The second great mystery of Sacajawea's life is that of her destiny after the Lewis and Clark Expedition. There are two distinct theories on Sacajawea's fate.

By 1809, as promised, Charbonneau and Sacajawea had brought Jean Baptiste to Clark in St. Louis. Charbonneau received a land grant from Clark and made attempts at living a domesticated life. All failed, as he was always drawn back to the frontier. He left St. Louis in 1811, leaving Jean Baptiste with William Clark. The couple next appears in the journals of explorer Henry Brackenridge, who recorded the presence of Charbonneau and "his wife, an Indian woman of the Snake Nation, both of whom accompanied Lewis and Clark to the Pacific."

Charbonneau then became an employee of Manuel Lisa, a fur trader who built Fort Manuel, just south of the border between North and South Dakota. John C. Luttig, the clerk at Fort Manuel, recorded the following on December 20, 1812: "This evening the wife of Charbonneau, a Snake squaw, died of a putrid fever. She was a good and the best woman in the fort, aged about 25 years. She left a fine infant girl."

By March of 1813 the fort had been abandoned due to attacks by the Sioux, who later burned it. The grave of this unnamed wife of Charbonneau has never been located. The clerk, Luttig, took the baby girl, Lizette, to St. Louis, where he had himself appointed guardian for her as well as for Toussaint, a boy of about ten years of age. Shortly afterward the name

William Clark was substituted in the court records as guardian for the two children.

During the mid-twentieth century, a journal kept by Captain Clark between the years 1825 and 1828 was discovered. In it he listed the members of the expedition and what had become of them. Next to the name "Secarjaweau," Clark made the notation "Dead."

The Shoshone people tell a different story. According to the Shoshone, Sacajawea left Charbonneau after a dispute with one of his new Indian wives. She spent time among the Comanche, where she married and had five children. Upon the death of her Comanche husband, she set out to return to her tribe, arriving at Fort Bridger, Wyoming, around 1843. Here she was reunited with her natural son, Baptiste, by then a noted frontiersman and western guide, and her adopted son, Bazil.

This woman, called *Porivo*, or "Chief," commanded great respect of both Indians and the whites who knew her. She spoke French and had intimate knowledge of the details of the Lewis and Clark Expedition. Although she rarely volunteered information, when asked, she stated that she had traveled with the white men to the big waters in the west and that Baptiste was the baby she had carried on her back during the expedition. She referred to her French husband as "Schab-a-no."

F. G. Burnett, an agent on the Shoshone Reservation at Wind River, Wyoming, in 1871, provides one such account:

> I remember very distinctly that one day about 1872 a group of us including Doctor James Irwin, Charlie Oldham, some other white men, and a group of Indians were sitting in a circle with Sacajawea. She was talking about her trip across the mountains, telling her story in the English language. . . . She told that when she was

out across the mountains with the Lewis and Clark people, word came to camp one day that a big fish had been found on the great sea, and that she begged the white men to allow her to go down and see the fish. She told about the fish she had seen . . . indicated [the size] by a space that [the whale] was from fifty to sixty feet.

Mrs. James Irwin, wife of another agent on the reservation, interviewed Porivo at length and prepared a manuscript containing her testimony about the Lewis and Clark Expedition. A fire at the agency destroyed this manuscript, but both Dr. and Mrs. Irwin were convinced that Porivo was Sacajawea of the Corps of Discovery.

Porivo lived to be an old woman on the Wind River Reservation, where she died on April 9, 1884, and was buried in the cemetery there. The Reverend John Roberts officiated at the funeral and noted in church records the death of "Bazil's mother." Originally, only a small wooden plank marked the grave, but in 1909 a cement marker was placed on the grave by the Shoshone agent and Porivo's descendants, with the help of a local benefactor. The marker is inscribed:

SACAJAWEA. DIED APRIL 9, 1884. A GUIDE WITH THE LEWIS AND CLARK EXPEDITION 1805–1806. IDENTIFIED, 1907 BY REV. J. ROBERTS WHO OFFICIATED AT HER BURIAL.

Professor Grace Hebard, of the University of Wyoming, dedicated thirty years of her life to proving that the woman who lay buried on the Wind River Reservation was indeed Sacajawea. Hebard published numerous accounts by both whites and Indians of encounters with Sacajawea during her later life, including those of people who had seen the medal given to her by Lewis and Clark. The testimony makes a compelling case for identifying Porivo as Sacajawea. The Bureau of American Ethnology accepted Ms. Hebard's conclusions.

After Luttig's account of the death at Fort Manuel was published in the 1920s, Dr. Charles A. Eastman, a Santee Sioux, was hired by the Bureau of Indian Affairs (BIA) to determine the true identity of Sacajawea. Bazil, who died in 1886, had been buried with "important papers" provided to his mother by the white leaders. Dr. Eastman exhumed the grave of Bazil in order to obtain these papers. To his dismay a leather wallet was found that contained documents that had so deteriorated as to be unreadable. Still, based on testimony and evidence collected, Eastman reported to the BIA on March 17, 1925, that he believed Sacajawea was the woman buried on the Wind River Reservation in Wyoming.

With Charbonneau's propensity to marry Indian women, either woman could have been another of his Shoshone wives who had knowledge of the expedition. Perhaps modern DNA testing may someday solve this mystery. Until then we must choose which version we find most likely to be true. Sacajawea remains Wadze-wipe, the lost woman of the Lemhi Shoshone.

ELIZA HART SPALDING
1807–1851

ELIZA SPALDING WARREN
1837–1919

"In the Name of Jesus Christ and Mrs. Spalding"

*T*he young missionary mother was home alone with her baby when she noticed the riders approaching on horseback. Several Indian men rode up to the crude log cabin and called out to her. Eliza opened the door. There was no cause for alarm; Indian visitors were an everyday occurrence at the Spalding home. Her husband, Henry, and their two oldest children were on a trip to the Willamette Valley, hundreds of miles away from their Lapwai home.

Eliza recognized the callers as members of a renegade faction of the tribe. With menacing gestures the Indians began demanding immediate payment from Eliza for corn they claimed had been trampled by the Spaldings' cattle. The lone pioneer woman was not intimidated, and she declined to pay. The riders became angry, threatening to kill Mrs. Spalding and her baby and to burn the house down around their dead bodies. Instructing the Indians to do as they pleased, she refused their demands and proceeded to calmly shut the cabin door. No repercussions ensued from this brave woman's actions.

Spalding cabin with Indian tepees nearby, 1836

This incredible bravery shown in the face of such danger earned Eliza Spalding the respect of the Nez Perce tribe. William Gray, a lay minister and handyman to the missions, wrote of her:

> She never appeared to be alarmed or excited at any difficulty, dispute, or alarms common to the Indian life around her. She was considered by the Indian men as a brave, fearless woman, and was respected and esteemed by all. Though she was frequently left for days alone, her husband being absent on business, but a single attempted insult was ever offered her. Understanding their language, her cool, quick perception of the design enabled her to give so complete and thorough a rebuff to the attempted insult, that, to hide his disgrace, the Indian offering it fled from the tribe, not venturing to remain among them. In fact, a majority of the tribe

were in favor of hanging the Indian who offered the insult, but Mrs. Spalding requested that they would allow him to live, that he might repent of his evil designs and do better in the future.

With her husband, Henry Harmon Spalding, Eliza Hart Spalding ran the most successful Protestant mission in the entire Oregon Territory, which included present-day Idaho, Washington, and Oregon. The impact of the Spaldings is still felt among the Nez Perce at Lapwai, Idaho, many of whom escaped the turmoil, fighting, and forced internment on reservations that their neighboring bands, such as Chief Joseph's band in the Wallowa Valley, endured. Although there was dissension in the last four years of the Spalding Mission, Henry and Eliza were far more successful in their work with the natives than their counterparts, Marcus and Narcissa Whitman, were with their mission at Waiilatpu.

The oldest of six children born to Captain Levi and Martha Hart, Eliza was born in Berlin, Connecticut, on August 11, 1807. Captain Hart, a farmer, moved his family to Holland Patent, New York, when Eliza was thirteen years old. As a farmer's daughter, she learned many skills that would serve her well on the western frontier. She was taught to sew, spin, and weave; to make soap, candles, butter, and cheese; and to cook over an open fire. Her hobbies included drawing and painting, which she did with some degree of talent. Eliza received formal education at a seminary for young women in Clinton, New York. After graduation from the academy, she taught school in Oneida County.

Although not raised in a particularly religious home, Eliza felt called to religion and joined the Presbyterian Church of Holland Patent at the age of nineteen. From then on this pious young woman lived her life devoted to God. When she was twenty-three, Eliza received a letter from a friend in Prattsburg, New York, informing her of a twenty-seven-year-old college student named Henry Spalding who wished to correspond with a pious young lady. Through a series of letters sent over the course of a year, Henry and Eliza developed a strong friendship. The two first met in person in the fall of 1831.

Henry Spalding was an illegitimate child, born in a log cabin in Bath, New York, on November 26, 1803, and raised in a foster home until he ran away at the age of seventeen. He then lived with a teacher until he was twenty-one, working for his board and education. Henry joined the Presbyterian Church at Prattsburg, New York, in 1825, at the age of twenty-two. That same year he enrolled in Franklin Academy. After a year, short on funds, Henry dropped out of the academy and began teaching school. Responding to a call for Christian missionaries to work in "foreign" lands, Henry returned to school with the goal of becoming a minister.

While in Prattsburg, Henry courted Narcissa Prentiss, the daughter of a local judge. Finding himself rejected by Narcissa, Henry became engaged to another church member, Levina Linsley. The two shared a dream of becoming foreign missionaries until Levina's health failed her, and she urged Henry to find someone more suitable for work in the missionary field. It was then that Henry began corresponding with Eliza Hart.

In the fall of 1831, Henry transferred to Hamilton College in Clinton, New York, and was formally introduced to his pen pal, Eliza Hart. Unhappy at Hamilton College, Henry next enrolled at Western Reserve College in Hudson, Ohio. On a return visit to New York in 1832, Henry proposed to Eliza and convinced her to return to Ohio with him. Within a year Eliza and Henry wrote to Eliza's parents asking permission to marry in Ohio rather than return home for their wedding. The Spaldings were married in the college chapel in Ohio on October 13, 1833.

As Henry's fiancée, Eliza attended an Ohio women's college; as Henry's wife, Eliza would be allowed to attend his new college, Lane Theological Seminary in Cincinnati, as a nonmatriculated student. When they married, however, Henry lost all of the financial aid he had been receiving, so the ever-industrious Eliza opened a boarding-house and pursued tutoring and teaching positions while Henry worked in a print shop to help pay for tuition.

After two years of theological training, Henry applied to the American Board of Commissioners for Foreign Missions for a missionary position among the Indians. In one of Henry's letters of recommendation, high praise was given to Eliza by the Reverend Bullard, who wrote, "His wife is very highly respected and beloved by a large circle of friends. . . . She is one of the best women for a missionary's wife with whom I am acquainted."

Henry's ordination took place August 27, 1835, within days of his appointment to work among the Osage tribe in what is now western Missouri. There was, however, one impediment to the fulfillment of the Spaldings' goal to work among the Indians— Eliza was six months pregnant. On October 24, 1835, Eliza gave birth to a stillborn baby girl. This caused her much grief as well as "protracted and severe" illness, according to her husband.

That winter Marcus Whitman, a physician who had been assigned as a missionary to the Oregon country, was desperately searching for associates to accompany him and his soon-to-be bride over the Rocky Mountains. Whitman's intended bride was Narcissa Prentiss, the very same woman who had curtly rejected Henry's proposal of marriage. Whitman needed to leave the East before the end of February in order to meet up with the American Fur Company caravan, which would, by their sheer numbers (hundreds of men and livestock), safely escort the Whitman party over the Rocky Mountains. Time was running out to find a suitable associate.

Henry and Eliza visited the Hart family for several weeks before embarking on their journey to the Osage tribe. Captain Hart, not a religious man, was opposed to his daughter's intended vocation and unsettled destination, but opposed as he was, Captain Hart gave the couple money and provided them with a brightly painted blue and yellow wagon. Probably sensing this would be the last time he would ever see his eldest child, Captain Hart traveled with the Spaldings as far as Prattsburg. Eliza's farewells to her family in New York, and later to her father, were filled with emotion. With the exception of her younger brother, Horace, who migrated west in 1846, Eliza would never see her family again.

In Prattsburg, on February 14, 1836, Dr. Whitman caught up with the Spaldings, whom he had been chasing in a desperate attempt to convince them to change their destination. Whitman implored Henry to come with him, saying that should Spalding refuse, the mission to the Rocky Mountains would be abandoned for another year. Although he questioned going into the wild with Narcissa Prentiss, Henry left the ultimate decision to Eliza. After praying privately about the matter for ten minutes, she "appeared with a beaming face" and announced, "I have made up my mind to go."

Anticipating final approval from the Board of Foreign Missions, the Spaldings agreed to wait for the Whitmans in Cincinnati. Eliza's diary entry of March 1, 1836, describes their mode of travel: "We have at length after a tedious journey of two weeks by land carriage arrived at Pittsburgh, where we intend taking a steam boat for Cincinnati." Eliza and Narcissa Whitman met for the first time when the Whitmans arrived in Cincinnati on March 17. Five days later the two couples embarked on their 3,000-mile odyssey to the land beyond the Rocky Mountains. They were joined by three missionaries en route to the Pawnee tribe. Also with them were two Nez Perce boys, John Ais and Richard Tackitonitis, whom Whitman had brought east with him from the Green River Rendezvous in present-day Wyoming. The party of nine missionaries traveled by boat to Liberty, Missouri, where they awaited the arrival of an American Fur Company steamboat to take them to Council Bluffs, where they would meet up with the Fur Company caravan. While awaiting the steamer at Liberty, the group was joined by William Gray, who told them he had been appointed by the American Board of Foreign Missions to travel with them as a handyman. Mr. Spalding, Gray, the Nez Perce boys, and two hired men left Dr. Whitman, the Pawnee missionaries, and the women in order to drive the horses and cattle they had purchased to Council Bluffs. One of the Pawnee-bound missionaries, Mrs. Satterlee, who had been ill most of the journey, died. While the group was conducting funeral services for Mrs. Satterlee, the American Fur Company steamer passed Liberty without stopping.

The group set out on horseback to join Spalding and Gray and catch up to the Fur Company caravan. Since the tents had been sent ahead with the wagons and livestock, the women spent several nights sleeping under the stars with nothing but a blanket over them. Urgent as the need to overtake Spalding and their supplies was, the pious group refused to travel on the Sabbath. Nearly two weeks after being left at the dock by the steamer, the group was reunited near Leavenworth. Dr. Whitman wrote back to the board from Leavenworth that he had doubts about Mrs. Spalding's health and her ability to withstand the long journey. Eliza was no doubt still feeling the effects of having given birth to a stillborn child the previous fall.

The party then learned that the American Fur Company caravan had departed without them. Since it was thought to be unsafe for a small group to travel beyond the Pawnee villages, the missionaries hastened to try to catch the caravan, even consenting to travel on Sunday. They encountered a great deal of difficulty in crossing the Platte River, making multiple trips to transport their belongings across with one canoe made of skins that had been partly eaten by dogs. Nearly a month after leaving Liberty, the missionaries finally caught up with the caravan at the Pawnee villages on the Loup River, in present-day Nebraska.

When they set out across the Plains with the Fur Company caravan, the missionaries traveled at the back of the caravan, breathing the dust of the hundreds of men and animals in line before them. Once in buffalo country, the group dined on little else, which caused Mrs. Spalding to become ill. On July 4 the party entered the South Pass, a natural route through the Rockies. Since crossing the pass meant traveling on treacherous, narrow paths, the party had left their large wagon behind and kept with them the Spaldings' smaller wagon. Up to this point the women had the option of riding in a wagon or on horseback; now, the only choice was on horseback. At one time Eliza fainted and was laid out on the ground. Feeling she was dying, she implored, "Do not put me on that horse again. Leave me and save yourselves for the great work. Tell mother I am glad I came."

The leaders of the caravan sent a wagon back for her, and by afternoon, she felt much improved. That same day Eliza Hart Spalding and Narcissa Prentiss Whitman crossed the Continental Divide, becoming the first white women to do so. The men of the group erected a monument commemorating the event. In her diary Eliza noted:

> Crossed a ridge of land today; called the divide, which separates the waters that flow into the Atlantic from those that flow into the Pacific, and camped for the night on the head waters of the Colorado. A number of

Nez Perces, who have been waiting our arrival at the Rendezvous several days, on hearing we were near came out to meet us, and have camped with us tonight. They appear to be gratified to see us actually on our way to their country.

On the evening of July 6, the caravan arrived at the American Rendezvous, a trading camp populated by 1,500 hunters, trappers, and Indians. That year's rendezvous was held in an extensive valley in the forks formed by Horse Creek and the Green River. "Were met by a large party of Nez Perces, men, women, and children. The women were not satisfied short of saluting Mrs. W. and myself with a kiss," wrote Mrs. Spalding. Each party selected their own campgrounds, guarding their own animals and goods. In spite of a parade of whooping Indians in full regalia welcoming them, "Mrs. Spalding was quite feeble, and kept [to] her tent most of the time," wrote Gray,

> The Indians would pass and repass the tent, to get a sight of the two women belonging to the white men. Mrs. Spalding, feeble as she was, seemed to be the favorite with the Indian women; possibly from that fact alone she may have gained their sympathy to some extent. . . . Mrs. Spalding's rest from the fatigues of the journey soon enabled her to commence a vocabulary of the Indian language. . . . [Mrs. Whitman] did not acquire the native language as fast as Mrs. Spalding, who showed but little attention to any one except the natives and their wives.

The American Fur Company caravan went only as far as the Rendezvous. Though the Nez Perce wanted to escort the missionaries on their preferred route, the missionaries chose to travel an easier path with a party of Hudson's Bay Company men who had arrived from Vancouver. The group was escorted to Fort Hall by members of the Flathead, Nez Perce, and Snake tribes. There they parted company, the Hudson's Bay men taking their preferred route west.

Eliza described the route taken by the missionaries as "rugged . . . dreary, rough and barren." The horse she was riding stepped on a hornet's nest, throwing her to the ground and dragging her some distance when her size-five foot stuck in the stirrup. She suffered no ill effects and was well enough to cross the Snake River a week later.

The route included narrow, winding, mountain trails through which Dr. Whitman insisted on taking the Spaldings' light wagon. The group was forced to dispose of some of their belongings to lighten the load, and Whitman removed two of the wagon's wheels, making it into a cart. With their animals failing and the route through the Blue Mountains said to be impassable for the wagon, Whitman left the contraption at Fort Boise (Snake Fort) with every intention of returning for it.

On September 1, 1836, the Whitmans arrived at Fort Walla, and the Spaldings came with the livestock on September 3. Following a brief stay there, the missionaries traveled the Columbia River to Fort Vancouver to meet with Dr. McLoughlin, chief factor of the Hudson's Bay Company. They intended to obtain supplies at Fort Vancouver, as well as present Dr. McLoughlin with a letter from the U.S. Secretary of War. It was crucial to have the blessing of the Hudson's Bay Company to settle in their domain.

While at Fort Vancouver, it was decided that Whitman would establish a station among the Cayuse tribe near Fort Walla Walla, and Spalding would build his station among the Nez Perce,

125 miles to the east along the Clearwater River in present-day Idaho. Although invited to spend the winter at Fort Vancouver, the wives agreed to stay only as long as it took their men to situate themselves at their new stations. Spalding returned for the women a month later.

The Spaldings and Mrs. Whitman arrived back at Fort Walla Walla on November 13, 1836. Eliza described the trip: "Reached this post yesterday, after a protracted and tedious journey up the Columbia. The terrific rapids, whirlpools and current on this river, makes a journey up from Vancouver very undesirable to me."

A party of 150 Nez Perce met the Spaldings at Fort Walla Walla to escort them to their new home at Lapwai, meaning "place of butterflies." The Spaldings arrived in the Lapwai Valley on November 29, 1836, and they lived in an Indian lodge made of buffalo skins for nearly a month while their log cabin was being constructed. The cabin was built entirely by Nez Perce men at the direction of Spalding and Gray. Within a year the Spaldings began construction on a new home on the banks of the Clearwater River near Lapwai Creek. The Spaldings' mission home was known as Lapwai, but when the U.S. government established a military post 4 miles up the creek in 1890 and named that Lapwai, the old mission site became known as Spalding.

Before a church could be built, worship services were held outdoors. It was winter, and the heads of those in attendance were often covered with snow before the service concluded. The weather, however, did not daunt the Nez Perce people, who were eager to learn from the Spaldings. "We might as well hold back the Sun in his march through the heavens, as hold back the minds of this people from religious inquiries," stated Henry.

The first two Nez Perce baptized by Henry were chiefs, Joseph and Timothy. Joseph, later referred to as Old Joseph, was the father of the famous Chief Joseph of the Nez Perce

Resistance. Timothy was a lifelong devotee of the Spaldings and rendered valuable aid to soldiers during the Indian wars of the mid-1800s. Chief Timothy ended all of his mealtime prayers with the phrase, "In the name of Jesus Christ and Mrs. Spalding."

Eliza opened her school on January 27, 1837, to pupils of all ages. Since she had no books, Eliza hand-printed her own primers. It was not uncommon for hundreds of students to show up for class. Due to the sheer number, Eliza taught them by first teaching a small group, then having that group recite the lesson to the next group. This teaching style worked well with the Nez Perce hierarchy. While the Cayuse were offended by the Whitmans' style of teaching chiefs and slaves together, the Spaldings were always careful to pay appropriate attention to tribal chiefs and leaders. Henry described the school:

> . . . two hundred and twenty-five in daily attendance, half of which are adults. Nearly all the principal men and chiefs in this vicinity, with one chief from a neighboring tribe, are members of the school. Their improvement is astonishing, considering their crowded condition, and only Mrs. Spalding, with her delicate constitution and her family cares, for their teacher.

In addition to her classroom duties, Eliza assembled a group of girls in her home twice a week to learn sewing skills. She found her pupils quite adept and willing to learn. Her artistic talent was invaluable in illustrating biblical passages through watercolor paintings. Eliza was dedicated to the Nez Perce people and truly enjoyed her calling. Once asked by a visitor to Lapwai if she ever got lonely, Eliza replied that she never found the time to feel lonely. Their associate, William Gray, wrote of her:

She was above the medium height, slender in form, with coarse features, dark brown hair, blue eyes, rather dark complexion, coarse voice, of a serious turn of mind, and quick in understanding language. In fact she was remarkable in acquiring the Nez Perce language, so as to understand and converse with the natives quite easily by the time they reached their station at Lapwai. She could paint indifferently in water-colors, and had been taught, while young, all the useful branches of domestic life; could spin, weave, and sew, etc.; could prepare an excellent meal at short notice; was generally sociable, but not forward in conversation with or in attentions to gentlemen. In this particular she was the opposite of Mrs. Whitman. With the native women Mrs. Spalding always appeared easy and cheerful, and had their unbounded confidence and respect. She was remarkable for her firmness and decision of character in whatever she or her husband undertook.

By spring the Spaldings had planted two acres of peas, seven bushels of potatoes, a variety of vegetables, and apple trees. Many of the Indians were cultivating the same. The mission included a small herd of cattle, including a milk cow. During the summer of 1838, the Spaldings obtained eight sheep, beginning Idaho's sheep industry. Tribal members supplied the couple with wild game and salmon for a varied diet.

The Spaldings believed that they must teach the Nez Perce a "civilized existence" in order for them to become successful Christians. Controversial as that may seem today, they did have the best interests of the Nez Perce at heart and perhaps prepared them for the changes that the endless stream of emigrants would soon bring to their country.

Eliza and Henry took eight Nez Perce children into their home to raise, noting, "We find this people anxious to receive instruction and to have their children educated." On November 15, 1837, Eliza gave birth to the first white child born in Idaho— her daughter, Eliza. The Nez Perce loved the child, as Eliza wrote, "Little Eliza is a great favorite with the natives, both old and young, and they are so determined to take her into their own arms, that they sometimes almost rend her from mine, and frequently when I am busy about my work, take her from the cradle."

Years later, in 1884, when an adult Eliza Spalding Warren returned to Lapwai, an old, deaf, mute Nez Perce indicated to her in sign language how he had rocked her cradle and looked after her while her mother taught his people. Methodist minister Jason Lee described the situation:

> Mrs. Spalding was so oppressed with labor, that she could not have the society of even her own little daughter. The child was put in a rude kind of wagon in the morning to be drawn about by Indian children, while the mother was occupied with her domestic cares or the instruction of her Indian class, or in watching their garden and wheat field. . . . She had been left without husband . . . for two weeks in succession.

As little Eliza grew, she became as fluent in the Nez Perce language as she was in her own. She often served as an interpreter and was frequently her father's companion on his horseback journeys throughout the Northwest. At the age of nine, she was sent, with an old Nez Perce woman and a packhorse, on a three-day trip to the Whitman Mission, where she was to attend school. As Eliza later said, "That is the kind of confidence my father and mother had in the Nez Perces."

Three more children were born to Henry and Eliza Spalding at Lapwai: a son Henry, born November 24, 1839; Martha, March 20, 1845; and Amelia, December 12, 1846. Eliza also suffered two miscarriages and was frequently in poor health. The chiefs visited her often during her illnesses, expressing their grief. One chief said, "Could it be I would die in your stead that you might live to teach my people."

The first women's club established in the Northwest was the Columbia Maternal Association, started September 3, 1838, by Eliza Spalding as president, Narcissa Whitman as secretary, and the four other missionary wives then in the Oregon country. The initial meeting, held at the Whitman Mission in Waiilatpu, was the first and only time the group actually met. The women continued their "meetings" at their respective stations twice a month and agreed to read suitable literature on motherhood and child care, while praying for all the mothers and children of the association. A record book kept the names and dates of birth of twenty-five children born at the missions and the deaths of several, including the Whitmans' two-year-old daughter.

Henry traveled to Vancouver in the spring of 1839 to obtain a printing press shipped there by missionaries in Hawaii. Both Henry and Eliza had been at work converting the Nez Perce language into print. Now with the use of the first printing press "in all of Old Oregon," Henry and Eliza were able to print primers, hymn books, and religious passages in the Nez Perce language.

The first four years of the Lapwai mission were years of great growth. Henry had built a blacksmith shop and taught the men to farm and raise livestock, while Eliza taught the women to bake, spin, weave, knit, and sew. By the summer of 1843, an estimated 150 Nez Perce families were farming around the Lapwai Mission. The missionaries saw the pinnacle of their success from 1842 to

1843, when their classrooms were crowded with eager pupils; girls worked at spinning and weaving; a sawmill and gristmill were operating; and hundreds, and on special occasions up to 2,000, Nez Perce came to religious services.

By the spring of 1847, however, the climate had changed, and only a few devotees attended church services. White emigrants had begun annual migrations into the territory by 1842, causing mass disruption to the Indian way of life. Some factions of the Nez Perce had become dissatisfied with the Spaldings' teachings when they did not find the "great power" they expected from learning the white man's ways. A new Indian agent attempted to force a white man's code of laws on the Nez Perce, which succeeded only in diminishing the authority of the subchiefs, leading to disorder. A man of Delaware Indian descent arrived among the Nez Perce, telling them of how the Americans drove his people from one country to another until few were left. A mountain man married a Nez Perce chief's daughter and began to assert his influence, saying that the Spaldings should pay the tribe for wood, water, and land use. This same man, William Craig, surveyed a claim that included all of the mission property; he attempted to have his claim legally recorded but was unsuccessful. Still, Henry wrote that Craig was remarkably friendly, a hard worker, and a very accommodating neighbor.

Both Henry and Eliza were threatened with physical violence during this period of discontent. Classes at the school were disrupted, buildings and fences were vandalized, and livestock was mutilated. The school was closed in 1847 because of threats and intimidations of a few vandals who would throw rocks and spit through doors and windows. Some chiefs expressed regret to the Spaldings but told them that the "infidel party are too strong for them to manage."

The Whitmans were experiencing their own troubles at Waiilatpu. Dr. Whitman had led a wagon train of 1,000 emigrants into the territory that year, an event that was disturbing to the Cayuse. The emigrants brought with them a measles epidemic, which was blamed by the local tribes on Dr. Whitman.

Henry Spalding and daughter Eliza stepped into this hostile climate when they arrived at Waiilatpu on November 22, 1847. Little Eliza was to enroll as a student at the mission school that fall. Five days after their arrival, Dr. Whitman and Spalding traveled to Umatilla to minister and tend to sick Indians. While there, Dr. Whitman was warned of a plot against him, which caused such concern that he returned immediately to Waiilatpu.

On November 29, 1847, the eleventh anniversary of the Spaldings' arrival at Lapwai, Dr. and Mrs. Whitman and seven others at the Whitman Mission were murdered by a faction of the Cayuse tribe led by a recent migrant of East Coast Indian descent. Four more men were killed the week after the Whitman Massacre, and nearly fifty women and children were held hostage at the mission for a period of three weeks.

Ten-year-old Eliza Spalding was one of the hostages. Eliza described the outbreak of the massacre: "All over the place was heard at once firing of guns, the yellings and war whoops of the Indians." The schoolchildren witnessed their teacher's murder as he was dragged from the classroom, "struck down and killed." The children saw many murders, including Narcissa's, and were forced to step over the bodies left lying about the mission for days. Little Eliza, the only one at Waiilatpu who could speak the Nez Perce language (common to the Cayuse), asked if they were to be killed but received no response except for an icy stare. "I put my apron over my face. I did not want to see the guns pointed at us," Eliza later said. Because she spoke the language, little Eliza was called upon constantly to interpret for the Cayuse captors, causing her additional stress. "With the constant strain and suspense, I became so reduced and weak that I could not get up without help."

All bodies lay exactly where they had fallen for three days until a priest and his Umatilla assistant came to the mission and buried them. Eliza implored the Umatilla assistant, "If you see my father anywhere, tell him not to come here, for they will kill him sure if he does." One of the Cayuse captors stepped forward and told her that he expected to meet up with her father and intended to kill him.

Not 4 miles from Waiilatpu, the priest and Umatilla man, who were being trailed by the Cayuse who had threatened Spalding's life, met up with Henry. The Umatilla man warned Spalding, telling him to head for the fog-shrouded hills, hiding by day and traveling by night, until he reached Lapwai.

Meanwhile at Lapwai Mrs. Spalding was sitting in the kitchen with her three youngest children and several others, including her brother Horace Hart, when a stranger burst into the room. The man, bleeding from a gunshot wound, had escaped from Waiilatpu and, though he had never been there before, arrived at Lapwai on December 4. Mr. Canfield, the escapee, brought the first news of the massacre to Lapwai, saying, "Mrs. Whitman is murdered and your husband without doubt shared the fate of all the women and children who I expect are butchered." He believed that the Cayuse would soon be at Lapwai to continue the massacre.

With remarkable calmness Eliza replied that they must communicate all of this to the Nez Perce, saying, "Our only hope is the Nez Perces." Eliza immediately told the story to two chiefs and sent them to inform their neighbor, William Craig, of the events. She then sent Chiefs Timothy and Eagle to rescue little Eliza if she was still alive.

When Timothy and Eagle arrived at the Whitman Mission, the Cayuse had just finished murdering the last two men, whose mutilated bodies lay by the mission-house door. Timothy entered the home with a look of horror on his face and asked young Eliza, "Is that the way they killed them?" She answered, "Yes." Timothy proceeded to tell the girl that her mother had sent him to get her but that the Cayuse would not let her go. Further, the Cayuse threatened that if the Nez Perce attempted to take Eliza, they would hunt them down and murder them all. For the first time during the entire ordeal, Eliza broke down, weeping incessantly. Chief Timothy embraced the child, drying her tears with her apron, and in a faltering voice said, "Poor Eliza, don't cry, you shall see your mother."

At Lapwai a messenger had arrived and told Mrs. Spalding that Henry had escaped. Eliza and her household decided to take refuge at the Craig home, but because it was the Sabbath, Eliza refused to go until Monday. The next day, as she prepared to move from the mission, a party of Nez Perce rode up, led by a Nez Perce who had participated in the Whitman Massacre. After leaving Waiilatpu he had gathered up a band of discontented Nez Perce with the goal of performing another massacre at Lapwai. Fortunately, Craig was at Lapwai with a band of friendly Nez Perce. Eliza and her children were placed in a wagon and encircled by the guardian Indians. The threatening Nez Perce saw that if they harmed Mrs. Spalding and her children, a fight would ensue among the opposing Nez Perce factions. Eliza and her children were then escorted to the Craig home. The malevolent Nez Perce group proceeded to pillage and loot the Spaldings' home.

Into this scene Henry arrived, after having traveled incognito 120 miles from Waiilatpu, the last 90 on foot after losing his horse. Henry was weak, starving, his feet cut to pieces, and he was bitterly dismayed to see his home being destroyed and possessions stolen by members of his Nez Perce tribe.

At Craig's home two young Indian boys galloped up with

word that a stranger in desperate condition had been found at Lapwai. The Nez Perce woman who found Henry knew him well but could not recognize him in the state in which he was found. Eliza sent the two boys back to Lapwai to see if this could possibly be her husband. Around midnight the messengers returned and affirmed that the stranger was indeed Henry Spalding. The next day Henry was reunited with all of his family except his daughter Eliza, who was still a hostage at Waiilatpu.

When word of the massacre reached the settlements in the Willamette Valley, the Americans were eager for revenge. Henry wrote to ask the Hudson's Bay factors and priests to use their influence to keep the soldiers from coming, saying that the Nez Perce had pledged to protect them if they could prevent the Americans from coming to avenge the murders.

Peter Skene Ogden, head factor of the Hudson's Bay Company at Vancouver, was able to ransom the Waiilatpu captives from the Cayuse. On December 29, 1847, fifty-one captives arrived at Fort Walla Walla from Waiilatpu. The following day Henry, Eliza, and three of their children arrived at the fort after having been escorted more than 100 miles in the dead of winter by fifty armed Nez Perce.

Though they were overjoyed to see little Eliza, they found her "too weak to stand, a mere skeleton, and her mind as much impaired as her health. Had she been dead we could have given her up, but to have her a captive in the hands of those who had slain our dear friends, and unable to deliver her, was the sharpest dagger that ever entered my soul," wrote Henry.

Ogden had just loaded the refugees on boats and sent them down the Columbia River when a war party of Cayuse arrived at Fort Walla Walla demanding that Henry Spalding be turned over to them. Word had reached them that the Americans were on their way to avenge the massacre. The Americans were not successful in apprehending the murderers. Five Cayuse instigators were later brought to Oregon City for trial. In the spring of 1850, the five were tried for their part in the massacre, during which young Eliza had to testify about what she had witnessed at the Whitman Mission. Found guilty, the five Cayuse were hanged for their crimes.

The Spalding family settled in the Willamette Valley in January 1848. Henry ministered to the settlers, taught school, and served as a postmaster. Eliza suffered ill health in Oregon. The trauma she had endured, as well as the long, hard, winter journey from Lapwai and rough, wet ride down the Columbia took their toll on her health. She never recovered from the heartbreak of having to leave her mission and beloved Nez Perce people, nor did she find much purpose to her life in Oregon. Eliza did not blame the Indians for the Whitman Massacre and always harbored hope of returning to Lapwai.

The governor of the Oregon Territory presented Mrs. Spalding with a rocking chair in 1850, in honor of her being the American woman who had survived longest in the territory. Expressing regret at leaving four children motherless, Eliza Hart Spalding died of "consumption" three years after leaving Lapwai, on January 7, 1851. She was buried in Brownsville, Oregon.

Her daughter Eliza, only thirteen years old upon the death of her mother, took on the burden of caring for her father's home and her younger siblings, the youngest of whom was only four. At the age of seventeen, Eliza married Andrew Warren on May 11, 1854. As a young mother, she returned to the Walla Walla country to homestead.

Soon after arriving, Eliza was alone with her two babies when she saw a group of Indians, enveloped in a cloud of dust, approaching. Her first instinct was to run and hide, but it was too late. The Indians drew near, asking, "Is this Eliza?" Her fears melting away, Eliza recognized Old Timothy. He had come from

Eliza Spalding Warren

Lapwai when he heard she was near his country. The Nez Perce were excited at seeing her but saddened that she had forgotten all traces of the Nez Perce language. Henry was to arrive the next day, so the Nez Perce camped and waited for his arrival. Following a warm reunion, they implored him to return to them.

Henry returned to Lapwai in 1862 for a few years and again in 1871. He died there on August 3, 1874, and was buried near the spot on which the Spalding house had once stood. In September of 1913 Mrs. Spalding's remains were removed from Oregon and reburied beside her husband in Lapwai. In 1925 the

Presbyterian Church placed a marble monument commemorating the Spaldings' work over the two graves.

Eliza Spalding Warren visited her birthplace at Lapwai for the last time in 1909. She told a congregation of Nez Perce how proud she was of the Nez Perce name and to have been the first white baby born among their people.

In a tribute to her parents entitled *Memoirs of the West: The Spaldings*, written in 1916, Eliza S. Warren penned: "Father and mother never regretted coming to the Indians. Though the journey was a long and severe one, through a wilderness where there were no roads, over mountains and across wide, deep rivers. They were often hungry and many times weary. For five long months they traveled." Her sister Martha added "They took possession of the country as the home of American Mothers and the Church of Christ."

To people throughout America, Eliza Spalding Warren was known as one of the last living survivors of the Whitman Massacre. Writers and historians sought interviews with her because of her firsthand knowledge of Northwest history. The pioneer woman often gave speeches about her life and the struggles of establishing a church on the frontier.

Eliza Spalding Warren, Idaho's first "American baby," lived to be eighty-one. A few years prior to her death, Eliza wrote in the foreword to her book: "I write to you while the closing shadows gather around me. Believing that we will meet with understanding in the new country across the last Great Divide, I bid you greeting and God Speed."

She died at her home in Coeur d'Alene on June 21, 1919.

LOUISE SIUWHEEM
1800–1853

Angel of the Coeur d'Alenes

*W*ar cries echoed through the hills, warning of the approach of an enemy tribe. The peaceful Coeur d'Alene encampment was suddenly under attack by avenging warriors from the Spokane tribe. The Spokanes charged the Coeur d'Alenes, encircling them with vastly superior numbers well prepared for battle.

Seeing her tribe outnumbered and realizing her people had no chance to survive such a surprise attack, Louise ran to her tepee and grabbed the large wooden cross she kept there. Holding the cross above her head, the pious woman marched through the encampment, imploring her people to follow her. The parade of chanting Coeur d'Alenes, led by Louise, marched straight at their menacing enemies.

The Spokane warriors could not believe their eyes. The sight of this woman, bearing a cross, dumbfounded them and filled them with fear and awe. The men lay down their weapons and retreated in great haste, vowing never again to challenge the Coeur d'Alenes.

Louise Siuwheem

Legend has it that this pious, nineteenth-century Joan of Arc saved her tribe from certain death with her bravery and unwavering Christian faith on more than one occasion.

When a Nez Perce war chief sent an envoy by canoe across Lake Coeur d'Alene to challenge her tribe into battle, the people turned to Louise, a respected tribal leader, for their response. She sent word back to the Nez Perce chief that her people were Christians, not warriors; and, if the Nez Perce stayed on their side of the lake, the Coeur d'Alenes would not fight them, but if they approached, they would all be killed. Thus dissuaded, the Nez Perce chief took his war party and departed.

Although there is no way to verify them, these legends have been passed along throughout the years. Stories state that Coeur d'Alene chiefs respected Louise Siuwheem for her wisdom and bravery and sought her counsel ever after and that Louise's intervention prevented much bloodshed between the Coeur d'Alenes and neighboring tribes. Louise held a position of great respect as the sister of the head chief, Stelaam, an iron-willed ruler whom many, including early priests, found difficult. Louise often acted as an intermediary on her brother's behalf, which may be the root of such stories.

Born around 1800, Louise was the daughter of a chief of the Coeur d'Alene tribe. They called themselves *Schitzu'Umsh*, but early French fur trappers, who found the people to be shrewd traders, sharp or hard-hearted like needles, dubbed the tribe *Coeur d'Alene*, meaning "heart of the needle, or awl." The chief's daughter was given the name *Siuwheem*,[3] or "Tranquil Waters," in the language of her people.

---

[3] "Sighouin" is the spelling used by Father De Smet and later writers. Father Connolly of the current Sacred Heart Mission spells and pronounces the name "Siuwheem," as it appears on her headstone.

Siuwheem was married when she was a teenager to a member of the Spokane tribe called Polotkin. The couple raised three sons. When her husband became crippled, Louise took on the role of provider for the family as well as nurse to her invalid husband.

Siuwheem's grandfather, the great Chief Circling Raven, had dreamed of a visit by two black-robed angels who descended from heaven to teach his people of a great spirit. This vision was passed on by Chief Circling Raven to his children and grandchildren. In April 1842 Jesuit priest Father Pierre-Jean De Smet, "the Saint Paul of the West," arrived among the Coeur d'Alene tribe. Father De Smet was the superior of the Rocky Mountain Missions when he met three Coeur d'Alene families who had traveled east on a buffalo hunt. The families had their children baptized by the priest and urged him to visit their tribe. Father De Smet was welcomed by the Coeur d'Alenes, but none received him so joyously as Siuwheem, who saw in him the fulfillment of her grandfather's prophecy.

Father De Smet described his initial impressions of Siuwheem: "Before her baptism, even, she was remarkable for her rare modesty and reserve, great gentleness, and a solid judgment. Her words were everywhere listened to with admiration and pleasure, and her company sought in all families."

Siuwheem and Polotkin were among the first of their people to be baptized. At his baptism Polotkin took the name Adolph, and Siuwheem took the name Louise, meaning "defender of the people." The priest sanctified the union of Adolph and Louise in the eyes of the church by performing an official marriage ceremony.

"Enlightened by a special grace," Father De Smet said of how Louise used her influence to induce many Indian families to follow her to the banks of Lake Coeur d'Alene to hear the priest preach the law of God. After her baptism Louise renounced all material wealth and pledged devotion to the priests, "I will follow the Black Gowns to the end of the world. . . . I wish to profit by their presence and their instructions to learn to know the Great Spirit well, to serve him faithfully, and to love him with all my heart."

In 1843 the Jesuits built a mission on the banks of the St. Joe River near the southern end of Lake Coeur d'Alene. During construction of the St. Joseph's Mission, Louise moved her family onto the grounds to be near the missionaries and "The Lodge of the Lord." Father Point became the mission's superior, succeeded by Father Joset in 1845. The Coeur d'Alene Mission was Father Joseph Joset's favorite mission; and, even after being appointed superior of the Missions of the Northwest, Father Joset chose to remain with the Coeur d'Alene people, making his headquarters on their land.

While still caring for the needs of her invalid husband and children, this frail woman, who was often in delicate health herself, spent all available time receiving instruction from the priests and sharing her knowledge and enthusiasm with other members of her tribe. The priests struggled with the Coeur d'Alene language. Father De Smet described his difficulty comprehending and speaking it even after many years working among the tribe. Louise offered the missionaries invaluable help in translating and teaching her people. She was given the position of tribal catechist, head teacher of the catechism, and devoted herself to religious instruction. Thus Louise became known as a great teacher.

In addition to teaching Louise took the position of defender of her religion. She was often at odds with the medicine men of her tribe who, fearing the loss of their own power, tried to disrupt the work of the missionaries. Frequently putting her own safety in jeopardy, Louise tirelessly worked to oppose the powerful medicine men. She boldly intruded upon them, entering their lodges uninvited, in order to lecture them.

One of the leaders of the medicine men was Natatken, a relative of Louise's who staunchly resisted Louise's teaching. Louise persevered, however, until she finally led Natatken and his wife and children directly to the priest to receive the sacrament of regeneration. Natatken took the Christian name of Isidore and became one of the most zealous members of the church, responsible for converting many of his followers to Christianity.

Louise also sought to ensure that once converted, her tribesmen did not revert to unsanctioned practices such as gambling. Chief Emotestsulem, who had been baptized as Peter Ignatius, became consumed by a prior addiction to gambling after his conversion. Upon learning of this Louise walked for two days to find the chief and return him to his duties as a tribal leader. Though it was contrary to tradition for an Indian man to publicly accept criticism and advice from a woman, this woman commanded such respect, even among men and chiefs, that she was able to convince Emotestsulem to renounce his habit and repent. Louise met each challenge with patience, courage, and perseverance.

This gentle woman harbored a special love for the children of the tribe, especially the young girls. Father De Smet wrote of her work among the children:

> By her motherly vigilance over the behavior of her children, by the simple and persuasive gentleness with which she treated them on all occasions, Louise had inspired them with the most profound respect and entire confidence . . . that . . . a single word from the lips of their good mother, was an absolute order, a law for them, which they accomplished . . . with eagerness and joy.

It was not uncommon for Louise to take in children whose parents could not care for them. Louise adopted two children who were unwanted because of their severe disabilities. One such orphan was Ignatius, a crippled, blind child who was stubborn, unruly, and a most disruptive member of the family. Though both children she adopted died at early ages, they received the same love and attention that Louise provided her own children, no matter how difficult their needs.

Louise Siuwheem's lodge became a shelter for young girls in need of counsel. She eagerly took them under her wing, offering guidance and instruction. In recognition of her endless work with children, she became known among her tribesmen as the "Good Grandmother."

This Good Samaritan was also an accomplished healer. Father Gazzoli (successor of Father Joset) said that he never arrived to administer to a sick or injured person that Louise was not already there ahead of him. She devoted herself to nursing the sick and dying no matter what time of the day or night she was called.

Although Father De Smet had intended for the St. Joseph Mission to be a permanent settlement, the yearly spring flooding of the St. Joe River raised havoc with the mission's crops. Father Joset decided to build another mission, which was started in 1848, on the banks of the Coeur d'Alene River about 12 miles east of the lake. The new mission was designed by Father Ravalli, who had visions of an elegant Doric-style church and grand mission. Using crude tools and makeshift supplies, the Jesuits and the Coeur d'Alene people set out to build the magnificent mission, a labor that was to take them five years.

Louise's leadership again proved invaluable to the priests when she convinced the tribal members to devote their labor to the construction of the new mission. Building of lodges was not seen as traditional work for Indian men, who scorned it as women's work. Louise offered high praise to those people who labored on the project and public criticism to those who refused to work. In the end more than 300 tribal members participated in the mission's construction.

The natural leader showed great managerial skills in organizing the labor of her people. Women and children were placed on teams and assigned such duties as cutting straw, mixing mortar, carrying water, and weaving grass mats. Built without nails, the church had a framework formed from giant timbers connected by willow bars and woven grass plastered with adobe, which formed walls a foot thick. The facade was later sided with wooden planks. Through the devotion and labor of Louise and her Coeur d'Alene people, the Mission of the Sacred Heart of Jesus was finished in 1853, where it still stands near Cataldo, Idaho.

In 1853 Louise became bedridden by illness, said to be consumption (tuberculosis). That summer she called upon Father Gazzoli to administer last rites. On her deathbed she implored her husband, Adolph, not to return to the home of his people, where there were no priests. Her dying wish was for her children to live good, spiritually rich lives and for those around her to join in one last hymn. Before the singing of the hymn was finished, Louise had passed away.

One of those kneeling beside the bed ran out crying. "'Siuwheem, good Siuwheem is dead.' The cry was taken up and echoed in the valley and the foot of the high mountains which encircle the Residence of the Sacred Heart," described Father De Smet in his writings on the life of Louise Siuwheem. A sudden desolation and grief went through the tribe as they mourned for a beloved mother and grandmother, a faithful friend, teacher,

PAINTING BY FATHER POINT, 1844

LOUISE SIUWHEEM POLOTKIN
c. 1800 — 1853

LOUISE WAS ONE OF THE FIRST COEUR D'ALENE
INDIANS BAPTIZED A CHRISTIAN BY FR. DE SMET
ON HIS VISIT IN 1842. SHE WAS MARRIED TO
ADOLPH POLOTKIN AND HAD THREE GROWN SONS.
THEY MOVED TO THE FIRST MISSION NEAR
ST. MARIES IN 1843 AND THEN CAME HERE WHEN
THE MISSION WAS RELOCATED IN 1846. LOUISE
WAS DESCENDED FROM CHIEF CIRCLING RAVEN
WHO HAD AN ANCIENT VISION OF THE COMING OF
BLACKROBES WHO WOULD BRING A NEW RELIGION.
GOD PREPARED LOUISE TO BE THE APOSTLE OF
HER TRIBE IN THE NEW WAYS. SHE TAUGHT
RELIGION TO THE CHILDREN, CARED FOR THE SICK
AND THE ORPHANS, TAUGHT HYMNS AND PRAYERS,
AND CAME TO THIS CEMETARY EVERY NIGHT TO
PRAY FOR THOSE BURIED HERE. LOUISE DIED AND
WAS BURIED HERE IN 1853 DURING THE
CONSTRUCTION OF THE BIG NEW CHURCH ON THE
HILL. THE MISSIONARIES CALLED LOUISE THE
SPIRITUAL DIRECTOR AND GUARDIAN ANGEL OF
HER WHOLE TRIBE.

Monument honoring Louise at the mission

translator, nurse, and social worker who led her people through peaceful times and war times and had lived in great poverty without ever showing her own needs or suffering.

Louise was buried in a plain coffin built by her youngest son and placed into a grave dug by her children. With a prayer and a personal farewell, each person in attendance at her funeral threw a handful of dirt onto the coffin. Her service was performed by Father Gazzoli, who believed Siuwheem to be "the spiritual directress, the guardian angel of her whole tribe."

On August 15 of each year, Coeur d'Alene tribal members make a pilgrimage to the old mission in memory of the good grandmother and the coming of the "Black Robes." Today no one is exactly sure where on the mission grounds Louise's grave lies. In 1985 Louise's great-granddaughter, Blanche La Sarte, and Father Tom Connolly had a monument placed at the old mission to honor Louise.

The Sacred Heart Mission, now more commonly called the Cataldo Mission or Old Mission, has the distinction of being the oldest standing building in Idaho. In 1975 the mission became an Idaho state park, officially titled Old Mission State Park. It stands today as a lasting monument to Louise Siuwheem and her people.

Jo Monaghan
1848–1904

Cowboy Joe

*T*he well-groomed mare trotted into town guided by her slight-statured rider. "Just another Eastern tenderfoot," noted the weatherworn prospectors and dusty cowpokes lining the sides of the crude main street. It was curious that this newcomer didn't carry a gun in this Wild West ruled by Colt and Winchester. Owyhee County's Ruby City was the center of Idaho's latest gold rush in 1867. Hopeful prospectors arrived every day, but there was something different about this one.

Standing barely 5 feet tall in his cowboy boots, wearing a baggy shirt, pants, and coat, this boy with the refined features and high-pitched voice would surely never last through the winter. Asked his name, the boy replied, "Joe Monaghan." It was not long before he was called nothing but Little Joe, due to the impression made by his appearance.

Little Joe purchased a pick and shovel in order to work the claim he had staked. The labor was grueling even for the most rugged of men, and Little Joe's hands were soon so blistered and bloodied he could barely continue working his claim. After giving

"Little Joe" Monaghan

up on prospecting, he took odd jobs and worked in the local mill; but whatever Little Joe did, he worked hard at it and won the respect of his tough neighbors.

Living in a rude Ruby City shack for more than ten years, Joe raised chickens and hogs. He made some money by keeping a cow and selling milk to the miners. Unlike the other men in town, Little Joe shied away from the saloons and card rooms, caring nothing for drink or dance-hall girls.

Feeling hemmed in by civilization, Little Joe took a job as a sheepherder and spent three years in this solitary occupation. With nothing but his horse and dog as companions, he tended his flock and fended off wolves through the long, snowy winters. After that Little Joe drifted between jobs, often working on cattle drives or wrangling and shearing sheep for local ranchers. Those he worked for described how the quiet cowboy never bathed or bunked with the other hands, preferring to lay out his bedroll under the stars alone.

Little Joe's only close friend was an older mine superintendent with whom he entrusted his hard-earned money for safekeeping. When Joe returned from cattle drives, he spent many an evening sitting on the porch of the superintendent's home shooting the breeze. It was a shock to everyone in town when the superintendent disappeared one day with Joe's life savings. The townsfolk, including Little Joe, formed a posse and chased after the thief, but nothing was ever seen of Joe's former friend or money.

A natural on horseback, Joe took to breaking wild broncs for a living. He became known throughout the Owyhees as a superior horseman. The *Idaho Capitol News* reported:

> No horse was too wild or savage that he could not be brought to saddle and bit under Little Joe's hands. To this day the countryside about Silver City and Ruby City tell of his remarkable ability in this line. Many a campfire is brightened by the stories of the little horseman and his prowess in subduing untamed steeds of the range.

A byproduct of riding the range was learning to shoot. Joe bought a six-shooter and practiced target shooting to try to develop his skill. Upon his return from one cattle drive, the locals noticed a marked improvement in Little Joe's shooting ability, as "he hit a can thrown in the air four out of five times, and was quick on the drop." Joe would say only that "some fellows from Texas" had been kind enough to show him a few tricks.

In the early 1880s Little Joe moved to Rockville and staked out a homestead claim about 10 miles west of town on Succor Creek along the Idaho/Oregon border. The foundation of Joe's log cabin was dug into the hillside, the low roof was covered in sod, and roughly hewn planks served as the door. His bed was a crude mattress filled with hay, which he shared with his horse during some sparse winters.

Little Joe loved the tiny town of Rockville, Idaho, with its population of twenty-one citizens. A civic-minded person, he voted in every election and served on several county-court juries. Although a bit withdrawn, Little Joe greeted his neighbors as they rode past his ranch and was well liked by all.

Before long Joe had dozens of head in his own herd of cattle and horses. One old-timer reported to the *Rocky Mountain News,* "He was a familiar sight along the banks of Succor Creek with his band of buckskin horses all branded with the familiar 'J.M.'" The 1898 Rockville directory lists one "Joseph Monaghan, Cattleman."

Whether for companionship or money, Joe continued to take jobs on other ranches. He was a familiar sight in the sheep corrals at shearing time, driving cattle, or breaking horses for his neighbors. During the spring sheep shearing of 1897, Joe was wrangling on the Otto Albert ranch near Payette. Otto and his neighboring sheep ranchers knew of Joe's skill breaking wild broncs and suggested that he ought to try out for a Wild West show. The ranchers arranged a meeting between Little Joe and Andrew Whaylen, a former member of Buffalo Bill's Wild West Show who was starting his own company.

Any misgivings he might have had must have been alleviated when Joe met Whaylen on the train platform in Iowa. Andrew

Whaylen, dressed in a fringed buckskin coat, was no taller than Joe himself. Andy advertised his show on the sides of three painted wagons he owned: WHAYLEN'S WILD WEST SHOW. THE GREATEST SHOW ON LAND OR SEA. Whaylen's Wild West Show featured Cowboy Joe, and $25 was offered to any man who could bring in a bronc that Joe couldn't ride. Little Joe was able to ride any bucking horse with ease, even horses that had thrown all the local riders.

Always the showman, Whaylen read a newspaper article about the Vitagraph Film Company that touted the moving picture as the coming thing. Whaylen wrote to the film company and suggested they film his show. Albert Smith of the Vitagraph Film Company was eager to accept the invitation, stating that this would be the first Western movie to be filmed west of the Mississippi. The show's star performer, Cowboy Joe Monaghan, was filmed on a bucking bronc, earning him a spot in film history.

Little Joe seemed uncomfortable with the spotlight, and when the Wild West Show closed for the season, he took the train back to his ranch near Rockville. Although Whaylen urged him to return to the show the next year, Joe refused, preferring to spend his time quietly at his ranch. His only companion on the ranch was a Chinese cook he hired to help around the homestead. When the old cook died, Little Joe appeared to shut himself away more than ever.

In late 1903 Joe was driving his cattle to winter pasture on the Boise River when he took ill. He was taken to the Malloy ranch for nursing, and the Malloy boys drove the cattle on to the river. Mrs. Malloy tended to Little Joe the best she could, but he had developed pneumonia, and in the first week of January 1904, Little Joe Monaghan lost his life amid a coughing fit.

Word of Little Joe's death spread throughout the valley, and neighboring ranchers came to the Malloys to tend to the body and build a coffin for their friend. The ranchers never could have imagined what they would find when they attempted to dress the body of this man who had voted, served on juries, and was the first western cowboy to appear in the movies. They found that Little Joe was really Little "Jo," a woman.

The tale of this woman who had spent nearly forty years living on the range as a cowboy not only stunned the local community but became national news. When the story was printed in Kansas, it was theorized that Jo may have been Kate Bender— "Kansas City Kate"—a saloon dancer who had murdered two people and fled Kansas, never to be seen again. Although headlines promoting this theory popped up in Idaho, those who knew Jo dismissed the idea.

Two plausible theories on Jo Monaghan's identity emerged from the rumors. The first centered around a neighbor remembering that he had mailed letters for Jo to a Walters family in Buffalo, New York. He wrote to the chief of police in Buffalo to determine whether Jo had left any heirs. Police Matron Anna Walters received the letter and responded. A Johanna Monaghan had been adopted by Miss Walters's mother. Johanna's mother had died when she was eight years old, and the stepfather left to raise the girl mistreated her terribly. At the age of fourteen, Johanna took her departure, telling the Walterses that she was going west to make her fortune. The Walters family received frequent letters from Johanna describing her work in mining camps and on ranches. Though she never told the Walterses she was living as a man, when Mrs. Walters asked for a picture of Jo, she was sent a head shot of Jo with very short hair, wearing a man's suit. Anna Walters even produced the photograph of a very masculine-looking Jo. This photo was printed in a Buffalo newspaper with the caption "Buffalo Woman Who Masqueraded for Years As a Cowboy Out West."

Another story evolved when neighboring ranchers went

DENVER PUBLIC LIBRARY, WESTERN HISTORY COLLECTION

Jo Monaghan debutante

through Jo's possessions after her death. The ranchers found photographs and letters between Jo and her sister in Buffalo, New York. The letters told the story of a Buffalo debutante who had been disowned by her wealthy family for giving birth out of wedlock to a son, Laddie. One such letter, dated September 11, 1868, was addressed to Josephine Monaghan, Rockville, Idaho:

Dear Sister,

I have lain awake nights picturing you in your wild wanderings and with your boy pressed tightly in my arms I have prayed to a merciful God to keep you safe and unharmed.

When I think of all my comforts and luxuries and then of my Josephine sleeping by night on a blanket and traveling by day with that crowd of rough men and uncouth women you describe in your letter I feel I cannot bear it.

I am glad you have decided to stay in one place, although the camp sounds so awful. Still, I know where to find you.

Laddie is sitting on the floor beside me. He had a slight cold last week but is quite well now. I hardly know how to live without him. I also am well and still longing for your return. It takes so long for a letter to reach me that I hope you will not delay in answering this one.

Your last letter was such a comfort. Goodbye now and with lots of love from Laddie and Helen

The series of letters painted a picture of a desperate single mother trying to carve out a living by working as a waitress at a restaurant on Broadway in New York City. Her son was born in 1866, and Jo had been abandoned by the baby's father. She had been forced, for a time, to put the baby into an asylum. When all of this became too much for the young mother, she placed the boy in the care of her younger sister and set out for the West.

It seemed from the tone of the correspondence that the child had been told his mother was dead. A later letter from Helen informed Jo of Laddie's graduation from Columbia Law School and subsequent admission to the New York State Bar Association.

There, among the faded letters that told the story of Jo

Monaghan's evolution from society debutante to Idaho cowboy, was an old daguerreotype of a lovely young woman making her society debut. Who could have guessed, upon the occasion of her "coming out" in society, that this beautiful, teenaged debutante would die a lonely Idaho rancher at the age of fifty-six?

Jo Monaghan's final resting place is a community cemetery on the Hat H ranch near her beloved Rockville. Her true identity may never be known.

JANE TIMOTHY SILCOTT
1842–1895

Gold Rush Princess

"One night three of us camped in a gorge far up in the mountains. When the moon began to shine we saw a bright light like a star gleaming out from the wall of a cliff. We were afraid. It was like the eye of the Great Spirit. In the morning we went to that place; it was a great shining ball like the white man's glass beads; we tried to dig it out. We could not get it."

Tales of rich veins of gold in the central Idaho mountains, such as the story above as told by a Nez Perce man in Byron Defenbach's *Red Heroines*, were often related by the Nez Perce people. In late 1859 one white man listening to the folklore equated the stories with gold and set out to pursue his fortune. Not knowing the route, he needed an Indian guide to lead him through hostile native territory into central Idaho. As no Indian man could risk the trek without arousing the suspicions of neighboring tribes, an eighteen-year-old Nez Perce woman volunteered to lead the first prospectors to the headwaters of the Clearwater and Salmon Rivers, thus beginning the great central-Idaho gold rush.

IDAHO STATE HISTORICAL SOCIETY

Jane Timothy Silcott

Princess Jane of the Nez Perce tribe was born at the mouth of Alpowa Creek around 1842. Her father was the great Nez Perce chief *Ta-moot-sin*, dubbed Timothy by the Reverend Henry H. Spalding. Timothy's mother was the sister of Chief Twisted Hair, the Nez Perce chief who had cared for Lewis and Clark's horses when they journeyed on to the Pacific via boat. Temar, sister of Old Chief Joseph, was Jane's mother. Old Joseph's son, the famous Nez Perce warrior Chief Joseph, was Jane's first cousin.

Chief Timothy's band was made up of the "lower" Nez Perce, who lived along the riverbanks; the "upper" Nez Perce bands lived above them in the mountains.

The Nez Perce called Jane by many names: The Princess Like the Turtle Dove, The Princess Like the Fawn, and The Princess Like Running Water. Princess Jane was slight of form, with lovely features and regal bearing. She was quiet and shy, while still brave and adventurous.

Chief Timothy was one of the Reverend Spalding's first converts to Christianity and a lifelong friend of the Spaldings. Timothy was sent by Mrs. Spalding to rescue her daughter, Eliza, from the Whitman Mission when she was a hostage there. On November 17, 1839, Timothy and Temar were formally joined in marriage by the Reverend Spalding. Chief Timothy was baptized at the Spalding Mission that same day. In accordance with his faith, Timothy brought his baby daughter to the Spaldings to be baptized and given a Christian name. Mrs. Spalding bestowed the name Jane upon the baby, and she was christened Jane Timothy. Jane's mother, Temar, with baby Jane strapped to her back in a *te-kash*, was baptized that day, May 14, 1843, and took the name Fannie.

Timothy named his village *Alpowa*, meaning "Sabbath Rest." With her family Jane lived between her main home in Alpowa and a tepee at the Spalding Mission. The lower Nez Perce encampment of Alpowa was in a valley below present-day Lewiston, where Alpowa Creek feeds into the south side of the Snake River.

Jane attended the Spalding Mission School, where Eliza Spalding taught her to read, write, and speak the English language. Eliza wrote of Jane sitting in her classroom by her sister's side. At a young age Jane was also taught by Eliza to cook, sew, spin, weave, make soap and candles, and keep house. Jane assisted with keeping the Spalding household.

Chief Timothy was often approached by neighboring chiefs who wished to arrange a marriage between the lovely Princess Jane and their sons. Timothy always deferred to his daughter, stating, "Jane has her own mind; she may choose who she will for her husband."

When she was around fourteen years old, Princess Jane married a man who was half Nez Perce—the son of a Nez Perce mother and white father. There was one son born of this union, who drowned in the Clearwater at a very young age. Her husband died within a few years of their son's death.

Chief Timothy had been a boy when he first encountered white men. On their return journey from the Pacific Ocean, Lewis and Clark and their party had camped at the lodge of Timothy's father on Alpowa Creek. During the visit, Lewis and Clark presented Timothy's father with a flintlock gun, which was passed on to Chief Timothy. According to Nez Perce history, Timothy's actions precipitated the arrival of white missionaries in the Northwest. Chiefs Timothy and Red Bear and their council had selected four Nez Perce men—Chief Black Eagle, Man of the Morning, No Horns on His Head, and Rabbit Skin Leggings—to travel to St. Louis in order to find Lewis and Clark and obtain the white man's "Book of Heaven." The arrival in St. Louis of the four Nez Perce seeking the Bible inspired the great western missionary movement of the early nineteenth century. In this respect Chief Timothy, the Spaldings' first convert, was responsible for bringing the Spalding Mission to the Nez Perce people.

When Chief Timothy heard that Sacajawea[4] had returned to her people, the Shoshone, he called Jane to his side. He asked Jane to ride to the land of the Shoshone to visit the woman he

---

[4] Indian people believed that Sacajawea returned to her people and lived to be an old woman. See Sacajawea chapter, page I.

remembered from the Lewis and Clark Expedition. The chief wished to send gifts to the great Shoshone lady. Princess Jane beaded a buckskin dress to bring as a gift of her own. She also brought beaded bags and a shawl as gifts from her father, and set out on horseback, leading a packhorse laden with gifts.

The Nez Perce princess found the Shoshone princess among the Shoshone people and presented the gifts to her. In turn Sacajawea gave Jane the buckskin dress she had worn on the Lewis and Clark Expedition. (Some historians dispute that this could have been the dress worn on the expedition, but the Nez Perce believe it to be a true account.) She also gave Princess Jane white glass beads strung on buffalo calfskin, which had been a gift to her from Captain Lewis. Sacajawea told Jane that President Jefferson had given Lewis the beads to present to the Indians as a gesture of peace and friendship.

Jane traveled back to the land of her father with Sacajawea's dress, necklace, her baby's neckpiece, and a lock of her hair. These items, along with a canoe used by Lewis and Clark, were put on display at the Old Spalding Log Cabin Mission Museum in the Spalding National Park until they were destroyed by a flood in 1964.

In 1858 during the Northwest Indian Wars, Lieutenant Colonel E. J. Steptoe brought his troops to Red Wolf's Crossing, near Jane's home, for his ill-fated expedition into the Palouse country. Timothy's fleet of canoes ferried the expedition of 159 men across the Snake River, and the aging chief is reported to have marched with Steptoe as a guide and interpreter. Steptoe's men were attacked in the Palouse country by more than 1,000 members of inland tribes including Palouse, Spokanes, and Coeur d'Alenes. Suffering heavy casualties, the expedition was able to escape during the night by leaving their tents pitched and campfires burning and taking an unguarded route over high plateau terrain, which Timothy had scouted. The chief led the men back across the Snake, and Jane and other Nez Perce women nursed the soldiers' wounds. Jane and her kinswomen gave the exhausted men water and fed them a breakfast of boiled salmon meat. When they were strong enough, the expedition returned to Fort Walla Walla. Colonel Steptoe later recorded accolades for Timothy and his band: "I had vast difficulty in getting the horses over Snake River which is everywhere wide, deep and strong, and without the help of Timothy's Indians it would have been utterly impossible for us to cross either going or coming."

Two years after the Steptoe battle, in 1860, a party of prospectors sought refuge in Chief Timothy's camp. Captain Pierce, the leader of the group, had heard the stories from the Nez Perce, which led him to believe that there was gold in the mountains of the Clearwater. On a trip Father De Smet made from Fort Boise to the Lemhi in 1844, he had observed, "These Indians roam over wealth that would make nations rich. Where I now sit I can see gold in the rocks." Pierce led his men as far as Alpowa on the Snake River, where he was met by hostile bands of Indians who threatened his life if he went any farther into their country. After several attempts to travel inland were met by armed resistance, Pierce asked Chief Timothy if he could winter near his camp.

Chief Timothy and his family members, including Fannie and Jane, held council with Pierce and his men. Pierce told Timothy of his plans, which he alleged did not include staying on the lower rivers. His plan, as he outlined it, was to follow the Lolo Trail into the land of the buffalo. Timothy told Pierce that all of the surrounding tribes knew of the white men's presence. Through his aid to the Spaldings and Colonel Steptoe, the older chief had raised the ire and distrust of neighboring tribes. He related to

Pierce, "My men and I are being watched every day; if one of us were to go with you it would be certain death." At that, Jane spoke out and volunteered to lead the prospectors into the mountains in the spring. She thought that by following the Colville Trail, which was not used by natives at that time of the year, they might avoid trouble on their way north. Jane knew the trail into central Idaho well; she had followed it many times with her people in search of camas roots and on their way to the buffalo country.

Pierce and the men began the journey by traveling up the Alpowa as if they were headed back to Walla Walla. After hiding for a day, the party retraced their steps to the Snake River, where Timothy's canoes took them across under cover of darkness. Traveling by night and hiding by day, Jane led the group across the Snake and up a ravine to a plateau above. She stayed to the right of the trail, using it as a guide, but taking care not to leave tracks on the path. They followed the present-day Washington/Idaho state line upland near what is now Moscow, skirted the Thatuna Hills, and crossed the upper Potlatch on to Elk River to Big Island on the North Fork of the Clearwater. They forded the swollen Clearwater and followed several more creeks until they reached Canal Gulch.

One of Pierce's men panned the first gold taken from Canal Gulch. Though the amount panned was worth only 3 cents, this find precipitated the gold rush, which brought thousands of miners stampeding into central Idaho. The prospectors returned the next year with more men and supplies and discovered additional rivers of gold. Since the gold panned was very fine, the prospectors named the creek where they found it *Oro Fino*, or "fine ore." The towns of Orofino, Pierce City, Elk City, Florence, and Warrens sprang up, followed by a rush to the Boise Basin. By March 1861, 500 men were bound for Pierce City.

Princess Jane returned to her father's lodge unaware of the sensation that would be created in the wake of the tidal wave of prospectors soon to arrive in her homeland. Alpowa became a way station for the ever-increasing stream of miners. Lewiston was established at the confluence of the Snake and Clearwater as a supply center for the prospectors. The old Nez Perce prophecy, as told through the mythical creature Coyote (often called "The Trickster" and an important character in Indian mythology), who was constantly saying, *Na-te-tam he-wah-yam* ("the people are coming"), became increasingly true. Tragically, Jane's oldest brother, Edward, was stabbed to death by a Cayuse man in retribution for the Timothy family's services to the white men.

Shortly after leading the Pierce expedition into central Idaho, Jane met John Silcott, a Harvard-educated man eighteen years her senior who had been sent to construct buildings for the government at Fort Lapwai. The couple was married by the Reverend Henry Spalding at Lapwai. A Lewiston pioneer described Jane: "She was a noted cook and housekeeper and made Silcott a fine wife. She was a good woman."

John and Jane Silcott made their home at the *Tsceminicum*, which means "the meeting of the waters of the Snake and Clearwater Rivers." The Silcotts built and operated the first commercial ferry in Idaho across the Clearwater. The couple often entertained travelers crossing the river. John was noted for his love of cards and drink, and Jane for cooking and caring for their guests.

A middle-aged Jane became plagued with rheumatism and attempted to ease the pain in her joints by applying the white man's medicine. John bought his wife liniment from a Lewiston drugstore for her pain, and she would sit beside her fireplace and rub the balm on her aching joints. But as one old-timer told it,

"The attempt to mix the white man's medicine with the red man's open fire met with disastrous results." Jane was fifty-three on January 17, 1895, when sparks from the open fireplace set her clothing ablaze, and she burned to death. Princess Jane was buried at the Tsceminicum, and a marble monument inscribed NOT FORGOTTEN was installed over the grave by her husband. When John Silcott died in 1902, he was buried next to the Nez Perce princess. The graves now rest in a privately owned wheat field and are tended by the people of Lewiston.

A bridge across the Alpowa and a state park west of Clarkston are named in honor of Chief Timothy. Within Chief Timothy State Park lie Silcott Island and the Alpowai[5] Interpretive Center. The site marks the original Alpowa Nez Perce encampment of the mid-1800s, which later became the now-defunct community of Silcott. All honor Princess Jane's family for playing pivotal roles in the development of Idaho and the Northwest.

[5] The Nez Perce tribe currently uses this spelling; however, the name remains "Alpowa" on maps and in historical references.

POLLY BEMIS
1853–1933

China Polly

*S*ounds of shattering glass and splintering furniture pierced the night air, replacing the lively chatter, shuffling of cards, and rolling of dice that had been heard only moments before. The high-pitched squeals of the dancing girls and the angry accusations slung about the room in both English and Chinese reverberated throughout the dusty streets of the rugged little mining town. Although it was but a typical western dance-hall brawl, the situation overwhelmed the shy new dancing girl, who at just nineteen years of age found herself in this foreign environment. Her instincts for self-preservation took over, and the minute ninety-pound girl darted out the back door of the dance hall and slipped through her neighbor's back entrance, seeking refuge from the melee.

This lively dance hall was run by the leader of the Chinese community—a handsome, statuesque man always seen attired in a Mandarin cap and silk brocade gowns. His hostesses were pretty, young Chinese imports whom he had purchased in San Francisco. The Chinese dancing girls were instantly popular with both the

Chinese residents and American miners living in the remote central-Idaho town. Racial tensions of the day combined with the nature of the business to create a volatile atmosphere in the dance hall that frequently erupted into violence.

The modest, young Chinese girl often sought to escape drunken brawls coupled with the rough treatment the girls sometimes experienced at the hands of their patrons by turning to her neighbor when these situations escalated. Although a professional gambler himself, the neighbor was an honorable, sober man, whose skill with a pistol assured the little dancing girl of protection each time she sought refuge from her place of business. Under these uniquely Wild West circumstances, a bond formed between the Chinese dance-hall hostess and the stern, quiet gambler.

Born to peasant farmers on September 11, 1853, in a northern Chinese river basin bordering Mongolia, Lalu Nathoy grew up poor. Her parents worked a small piece of land but could muster little to feed their family. Drought and raids by Mongolian bandits often robbed the farmers of the few crops they could produce.

In the early 1870s famine plagued the countryside due to a particularly severe drought. The crops that were grown that year were plundered by raiders from the north. The Nathoy family was in danger of starvation. To save the entire family from extinction, Lalu's father sold her to a raiding chieftain, who was also known to traffic in slavery. In exchange for his daughter, Lalu's father received enough seed to plant his next crop.

The slavery ring shipped Lalu from China to San Francisco, where an old woman smuggled her north to Portland for a wealthy Chinese man who had purchased Lalu for $2,500. An elderly Chinese man met Lalu in Portland and brought her by packtrain to the mining town of Warren,[6] Idaho. Here the tiny Chinese girl with bound feet was introduced to Warren as Polly, a name that

Polly Bemis in her wedding dress

would stick with her throughout her life in Idaho County.

Life was rough in remote central-Idaho's mining towns. The country was isolated, rugged, and mountainous—and made even more inaccessible by long, snowy winters. Gold brought a mix of inhabitants to Warren. When Polly arrived in town, in 1872, there were an equal number of Chinese and Caucasian residents, totaling 3,000 people.

Polly may have lived as her purchaser's concubine, a common Chinese practice of the day. A concubine served as a mistress but in China held legal status as a member of the family. Most accounts told by Warren's pioneers state that Polly was a hostess in her owner's dance hall. These old-timers liked to tell of Polly's actions when the situation turned too rowdy in her master's saloon and Polly sought refuge in a neighboring gambling establishment run by Charlie Bemis.

Charlie Bemis was the son of a Connecticut jeweler; he had come to central Idaho to seek his fortune in gold. Prospecting was difficult and dirty work, and Charlie was not the most industrious of men. Charlie found poker a more suitable vocation and started a gambling hall in Warren. Charlie's place was in a small building with a bar toward the front and a bedroom at the rear. Since Charlie cared little for alcohol, the bar catered to gamblers like himself. Roulette wheels and card tables filled the front room of the establishment.

Polly found her neighbor's lack of attention to tidiness unsettling. A hard worker who was constantly in motion, Polly occupied herself many afternoons with the business of cleaning up Charlie's living quarters. This did not go unappreciated by Bemis, who found himself increasingly drawn to the tiny dance-hall girl.

---

[6] The town was originally called Washington, then Warren's Diggins, later Warrens, and currently Warren.

How Polly paired with the educated Easterner is still a mystery and has become the enduring legend of "Polly Bemis–Poker Bride." Popular legend has Charlie Bemis winning Polly from her Chinese captor in a poker game. This story made Polly Bemis a legend, famous throughout Idaho.

On her deathbed, however, Polly denied this version of events, claiming that the real "Poker Bride" was an Indian girl named Molly. Perhaps the name similarity caused the confusion and intertwining of the tales of these two women. According to an early resident of Warren, Bemis did take Polly away from her Chinese owner but not in a poker game.

However it happened, Polly came to cohabit with Charlie Bemis, and theirs was a long and contented union. Polly operated a restaurant and boardinghouse in conjunction with Charlie's gambling parlor. Polly's reputation as an excellent cook and hostess with a fine sense of humor spread throughout the region and brought her many patrons. Another of Polly's talents was as an artist adept at goldsmithing. Polly fashioned gold nuggets into jewelry, charms, and trinkets, which she sold to the locals. She also had a talent for sewing and crocheting clothing and decorative items. With her many skills and industrious nature, Polly's hands were always at work.

Charlie's card games were famous throughout the region, and in 1890 this avocation was to threaten Charlie's life. While reclining on a bench in his establishment, Charlie was shot through the head by a young intruder. Johnny Cox, a man from Lapwai, was angry over a gambling loss to Bemis and shot him to settle the score. The local doctor proclaimed Bemis "too far gone" to be saved, but Polly refused to accept this death sentence for her mate. Polly removed the bullet from Charlie's neck, applied ancient Chinese herbal treatments, and nursed him back to health over a period of many months. Johnny Cox was captured and given a prison sentence, while Polly's nursing skills further endeared her to the community. Polly became the person that the citizens of Warren turned to for healing when they were sick or injured.

Polly and Charlie Bemis were married in Warren on August 13, 1894, by Justice of the Peace A. D. Smead (husband to "Molly the Poker Bride"). Their official marriage certificate documented the marriage of "Chas. A. Bemis and Miss Polly Nathoy at the residence of C. A. Bemis." The formalization of Polly and Charlie's nearly two-decade union was probably to ensure that Polly would not be deported under the new Chinese Deportation Act.

The Bemises purchased property on the banks of the Salmon River, where they built their ranch house. The Salmon River was called The River of No Return because once supply boats had made it through the river's rapids, they could not go back upstream. Originally called the Bemis Place, the ranch eventually came to be known as the Polly Place. In 1911 a nearby creek was named Polly Creek by a government survey team floating the Salmon River. The name was suggested to the surveyors by Polly's closest neighbors.

Although the river-canyon terrain was steep, Polly managed a flourishing vegetable garden. She supplied fruit and vegetables to the miners traveling the river, while Charlie operated a ferry. In addition to farming, tending to her beloved animals, and hunting with her husband, Polly loved to fish and compare her catch of the day with her nearest neighbors—two prospectors named Charlie Shepp and Peter Klinkhammer. As Charlie Bemis aged and became more and more incapacitated, Shepp and Klinkhammer looked after the Bemis ranch and aided in many of the day-to-day chores.

Two tragedies occurred in Polly Bemis's life in 1922. First, her beloved ranch home burned to the ground in August. The bedridden Bemis was helped to safety by Charlie Shepp. As Shepp wrote in his diary, "Got the old man out by the skin of my teeth." Sadly, Polly's faithful dog, Teddy, perished in the fire.

Polly Bemis in Warren, Idaho, 1923

The second tragedy occurred on October 29, 1922, when Charlie Bemis died of his ailments, possibly tuberculosis. Following Charlie's death, the grieving Polly was taken by friends to Warren to live.

In 1923, seeking medical attention, Polly visited Grangeville, Idaho, where she experienced her first automobile ride, picture show, and shopping trip for ready-made apparel and where she saw her first train. The following year friends took Polly to Boise to see the sights of the big city, including the elegant Idanha Hotel and high-rise buildings with elevators and electric lights. Charlie Bemis had told Polly they would never even see the railroad, but she experienced the wonders of modern society after his death. Although Polly enjoyed the sights of the city, she reported that it made her tired to see so much at once. Polly returned home to a newly constructed cabin built by Shepp and Klinkhammer. Now in her seventies and in need of assistance, Polly deeded her land and personal property to the two prospectors in exchange for lifetime care for herself and the ranch.

Polly weathered another ten cold, snowy winters at the Salmon River ranch until 1933, when she became seriously ill. Shepp and Klinkhammer carried Polly on horseback through treacherous mountain trails to the War Eagle Mine, where a nurse and deputy sheriff transported her nine hours by ambulance to the Idaho County Hospital in Grangeville. She died there on November 6, 1933, at the age of eighty-one.

Polly was originally buried in Grangeville; a marker for her grave was purchased by Peter Klinkhammer's heirs following his death. After her home was placed on the National Register of Historic Places and dedicated as a museum in June of 1987, Polly's grave was relocated to the Salmon River site. The museum displays many of the Chinese pioneer's personal belongings. The Polly Bemis Ranch is now a popular river-rafting destination.

POLLY BEMIS

In August of 1996 Polly Bemis was inducted into the Idaho Hall of Fame. This tiny, dark-eyed, former slave girl, standing barely 5 feet tall, or as Polly had said, "only as tall as a broom," captured the hearts of all who knew her with her natural charm and nobility. "Poker Bride" or not, Polly Bemis became an Idaho legend in her own right.

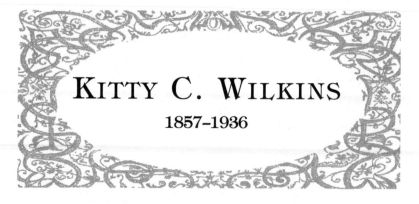

KITTY C. WILKINS
1857–1936

Queen of Diamonds

*N*othing could have prepared the two young cowboys for their encounter with the approaching rider. A golden palomino galloped up the dusty ranch-house road that late summer day. The horse's flowing yellow mane and tail were a perfect match for the rider's own flaxen mane. The startled cowboys stared in disbelief at the stunningly beautiful blue-eyed blonde coming toward them. After riding for several days along the border between Idaho and Nevada in search of work with a cattle outfit, the gorgeous woman before them seemed like an apparition.

Regaining his composure, the younger of the two asked, "Can you tell us where we can find the boss?"

"I am the boss," replied the woman firmly.

The two youthful cowboys had just met the legendary "Horse Queen of Idaho," Kitty Wilkins. Through her talent for raising and trading horses and penchant for garnering publicity, Kitty also earned titles such as "The Golden Queen" and "The Queen of Diamonds." The latter was a reference to her ownership of the Diamond Ranch.

The daughter of two western pioneers, J. R. and Laura K. Wilkins, Kitty was born in Jacksonville, Oregon, in 1857. Twenty-one-year-old J. R. Wilkins and seventeen-year-old Laura were married in 1853 in Fort Madison, Iowa, where he had moved from Indiana and she from Maine. Shortly after their marriage, the Wilkins couple joined a wagon train to follow the Oregon Trail west. They resided in Oregon City and then in the Rogue River Valley at Jacksonville, where Kitty was born, before moving to California. A gold rush brought the family to Florence, Idaho, in 1862. Kitty took great pride in the fact that her mother was the first woman to arrive at the gold camp. She said, "I feel that my brother and I can justly claim that our parents came to Idaho before any others."

After making several more moves in and out of Idaho, J. R. Wilkins settled his wife and children on a large spread in southern Idaho's Bruneau Valley. The Wilkins Island Ranch was located on land at the fork of the Bruneau River near Jarbidge Mountain, rather than on an actual island. The Wilkinses' holdings spread to other outposts along the Snake River, at Mountain Home and into Nevada. Their range was 75 miles away from the main ranch, stretching into the Owyhee Mountains.

Although her father had several thousand head of cattle and horses, Kitty always preferred raising horses to cattle. In addition to loving horses, the shrewd Miss Wilkins saw them as much more profitable, stating, "A 3 or 4 year-old steer. . . worth but $20, while a horse of the same age is worth $85–$100. . . horses are much more easily raised and do not require half the care."

Considering it romantic, Kitty loved to tell reporters about her start in the business. Neighbors bidding the Wilkins family goodbye upon one of their departures from Oregon gave two-year-old Kitty two $20 gold pieces. Her father bought the toddler a filly, and, as Kitty put it, "from the increase all of my bands have come."

Kitty was a gifted rider whose brothers taught her to shoot both pistols and rifles proficiently, "that being a necessary part of a woman's education out there [in the West] in those days." Kitty was sent to a private school for girls in San Jose, California, for her formal education and social refinement. She also traveled throughout the United States to all the major cities as part of her cultural enlightenment.

Upon returning to Idaho she was at first lonely, until she developed a taste for the family horse business. Kitty later expressed her feelings about Idaho and her business to an Eastern reporter, "Do I like living away out in Idaho? Oh, so much! I go out to roundups in the spring and fall and enjoy myself ever so much. It is a fascinating business and grows upon you."

When her father took young Kitty on one of his trips east to a horse market, she became hooked on the business of selling horses. From that time on she constantly accompanied her father to market his horses. Within a few years of that first trip, Kitty had developed her own distinct marketing plan and could sell horses better than her father. She was a shrewd businesswoman and an excellent judge of horseflesh. She prided herself on selling only high-quality stock. To one Midwestern reporter she boasted, "I bring the best stock to market that comes from the West. I never ship a blemished animal from the ranch. They are all sound when they leave there."

Kitty and her younger brothers eventually took over their father's ranch. While her brothers concentrated on cattle ranching, Kitty took over the horse outfit. No one ever questioned Kitty's authority or business sense. She was the undisputed boss of the Diamond Ranch.

Wild horses abounded on the range between Nevada's Humboldt River and Idaho's Snake River. These mustangs became the property of anyone who could catch and put a brand on them. Kitty saw a way to expand her own small herd, started with the purchase of the $40 filly when she was just two. She hired the best riders and set out to claim every unbranded mustang from the Nevada/Idaho line to the Owyhee River in Oregon. Kitty registered the Diamond Brand, a brand that was to become synonymous with fine horse stock, and set to work branding every wild horse she could bring in.

In addition to registering her own brand, hiring the finest cowboys available, and raising sound stock, Kitty marketed her horses in the most lucrative fashion. She bought stallions from around the world to develop her stock. Her lines included Clydesdales, Percherons, Morgans, Normans, and Hambletonians. After this she claimed to have "no native Oregon or Spanish horses" on her ranch.

Rumors put the Diamond Ranch holdings at 20,000 head of horses. In reality that number may have been closer to 5,000 head on the ranch at any one time. It took up to forty men during fall roundup to cut out and brand stock on the Diamond Ranch.

Kitty's marketing skills got her contracts with lucrative horse markets in the East and as far away as Dawson City in the Yukon Territory. One of her best customers was the United States Cavalry. At one point she was supplying six train cars of broke horses every two weeks to Eastern markets. Since each stock car held twenty-six horses, Kitty's hands had to break 156 horses for each shipment. Because the Diamond Ranch cowboys were breaking broncs continuously, they became known throughout the West as some of the West's most skilled riders.

Kitty C. Wilkins

Kitty Wilkins ran the "hardest riding outfit west of the Mississippi River," according to Harvey St. John, Kitty's youngest bronc rider and personal friend. Cowboys who rode with the Diamond Ranch were among the finest in the world. Buffalo Bill's Wild West Show hired some of the Wilkinses' horsemen; others became top rodeo champions. The young cowboy described riding for Kitty: "If a man weren't a good rider when he went to work for her, he was a good rider when he left or he wasn't riding at all—unless in a hearse."

The Queen of Diamonds ruled her cowboys with an iron hand. Although they were hard-edged, rough-hewn characters, some of whom became notorious outlaws, they respected Kitty, and her word was law on the Diamond Range. Any hand that disobeyed her was run off the range immediately.

The lovely horse queen caused an instant sensation when she arrived in the East to market her animals. As her obituary characterized it: "The sight of a beautiful, slender, young blonde, dressed in modish fashion, personally selling her stock, and knowing a complete knowledge of each horse's good points, created a furore [sic]." Citizens of the Eastern cities were awed by Kitty Wilkins's beauty and grace. She was interviewed wherever her travels took her. A reporter in St. Louis was stunned by Kitty's looks and so described their meeting:

> The reporter was hardly prepared to meet the tall young woman, dressed in a swell, tailor-made costume, her blonde curls surmounted by a dainty Parisian creation, who greeted him with perfect self-possession. One might be excused for imagining that Western ranch life would coarsen any woman, no matter what her natural tendencies might be, but one glimpse of Miss Wilkins

is enough to completely dissipate the idea. She is a strikingly attractive woman.

Meanwhile, a Sioux City reporter described Kitty as a

... tall stately blonde, with fluffy, golden hair, large blue eyes that have quite a knack of looking clear through one, regular features and pearly teeth which glisten and sparkle when she smiles, and she has a habit of smiling very frequently. Her lips are red and full, and her mouth and chin denote a certain firmness of manner, no doubt acquired in her peculiar calling.

San Francisco awarded Kitty their "Palm" for beauty when she visited that city. This was an honor bestowed by the local newspapers and reported in the society pages.

Being the most notable, if not only, woman horse dealer in the country, Kitty attracted a great deal of attention from the press. She was adept at public relations, promoting her fame wherever she went.

The beautiful Kitty never married. It is said that she loved only one man in her life—the Diamond Ranch's top foreman. He and Kitty were engaged to be married when the engagement ended violently. Kitty's fiancé was shot in a typical range dispute over a watering hole. Reportedly Kitty never showed a romantic interest in another man.

The end of World War I also signaled the end to prosperity in the horse market. Automobiles and machinery were taking the place of horses. Irrigation projects took over the once-expansive horse ranges.

Kitty saw the changes occurring and, already a wealthy woman, decided to retire from the business. She chose to spend her remaining years in a grand home in Glenns Ferry. People who knew Kitty claimed that her beauty never really faded. Even in retirement she kept abreast of current issues and progress across America.

A respected Idaho pioneer, Kitty was a guest of honor at the Boise Centennial Celebration. She headed the pioneer parade in a horse-drawn carriage. The horse queen's ornate saddle was put on display at the Idaho State Historical Museum, along with her portrait.

Kitty C. Wilkins died of a heart attack at the age of seventy-nine on October 8, 1936, at her home in Glenns Ferry, and was buried in Mountain Home.

Perhaps the passing of this notable pioneer horsewoman can best be described in Kitty's own words. When her brother and business partner, John, passed away just three weeks prior to her own death, Kitty reflected:

> The years are taking their toll of these early pioneers and few remain to tell us of the romantic beginning of the wonderful west we know. It is difficult for us, in our ease and comfort of present day surroundings, to conceive of the hardships, the privations and the suffering endured by these men and women that they might establish and build up a country for their families and those who would follow.

MAY ARKWRIGHT HUTTON
1860–1915

Hurricane May

*I*t was Sunday afternoon, and the portly boardinghouse proprietor found herself with a few rare spare moments. May took down her black lockbox and examined the contents—scraps of paper designating her the owner of shares and interests in at least two dozen prospects. Ever since her childhood in Ohio, May had dreamed of striking it rich. She came west to make her fortune in the mining district of Coeur d'Alene. As a cook, boardinghouse operator, and friend to the miners, May had invested in many prospective mines over her fourteen years in northern Idaho. Perusing the shares represented on these tattered slips of discolored paper, May knew them to be worthless, but still she gently wrapped them back up and secreted them away in her lockbox.

Just then there was a knock on the door of the small cabin perched on a hillside above the town of Wallace. Two acquaintances of Al and May Hutton had come to the cabin to ask the Huttons to invest in their mine, the Hercules. The two prospectors, Harry Day and "Dad" Reeves, would sell a one-sixteenth interest in the Hercules for $505, and Al could work off a portion of the assessments that would incur.

Examining ore samples inside the Hercules cabin, 1901

In 1897 the Huttons joined an odd assortment of investors in the Hercules mine: Harry Day, a bookkeeper; "Dad" Reeves, a barber; Gus Paulsen, a milkman; Harry Orchard, a storekeeper who would become infamous as a hit man for the mining unions and who later pled guilty to murdering the governor of Idaho; Al Hutton, a train engineer; and Al's wife, May, a cook and boardinghouse owner. Over the next few years, the Huttons would have the opportunity to add to their original shares. Investors came and went from the group, including Harry Orchard, who gambled away his interests. The core group of investors were all hardworking people who contributed endless labor to the mine.

Men and women of the group sat side by side in the tarpaper-lined shack at the mouth of the mine tunnel, vigilantly sorting specimens by candlelight. Many meetings between the shareholders were held in Al and May's cabin. May's contributions to these meetings usually included a hearty pot roast and succulent berry pie. Paulsen would describe the characteristics of the vein he was working and dump samples from his canvas bag onto May's bed (which doubled as a couch), spreading the sparkling galena out for all to admire. Not wanting to miss a thing, May could hardly keep her attention on her cooking. She went from the stove to the bed, leaving a trail in her wake as dough from her fingers dropped to the floor.

Twelve years after the mine was discovered, and four years after the Huttons became partners, on June 13, 1901, Gus Paulsen struck a vein of the richest silver ore ever found in the Coeur d'Alenes. The partners had struck it rich, although it took another three years for the Huttons to become actual millionaires.

May's rags-to-riches story began with her birth on July 27, 1860, in the coal-mining region of Mahoning County, Ohio. Born Mary Arkwright, she was the illegitimate child of an itinerant preacher and snake-oil salesman and Mary Bittenbender. May never knew her mother, who, either by death or desertion, left the child to be raised by her father, Asa Arkwright. When May was ten years old, her father removed her from school and sent her to live with his blind father as a caretaker.

Young May's duties were to cook and clean for Grandfather Arkwright and to guide him around town. Grandfather Arkwright had a keen interest in politics, and May led him by the arm to many a political rally. One such rally set May's life on a course of political activism.

One evening Grandfather Arkwright and his dutiful granddaughter attended a speech by a young Republican lawyer named Major William McKinley, who later became the twenty-fifth president of the United States and was assassinated during his second term. Grandfather Arkwright invited McKinley home to spend the night, and May passed the evening serving the men cider and home-fried doughnuts while she listened to them discuss the Civil War, Reconstruction, and women's rights. The future president patted May's head and told her that he hoped when she grew up it would be in "an enlightened age of equal suffrage."

Her grandfather was also an inspiration in her life, as she received no guidance from her father. But she did enjoy a warm relationship with her half-siblings from her father's legitimate marriage. May later told a friend, Idaho's U.S. senator William E. Borah, of a quote from her grandfather that seems to have provided her life's motivation: "Hitch your wagon to a star, girlie. You may never reach the eminence to which you aspire, but place no limit on your aspirations."

Typical of the time, though, Grandpa Arkwright wished May would find a good husband. At just eighteen years of age, the plain, plump girl was wed to Frank Day. There is no record of this marriage, or of what became of the union, but on June 6, 1882, at the age of twenty-two, May married Bert Munn, a mule driver for the local coal mine. Within a year of the marriage, Bert had disappeared with the couple's savings. Word came back that he had drowned following his flight from their home and the boardinghouse May ran.

Lured by the stories of riches from western gold mines and an ad placed by the Northern Pacific Railroad for the Coeur d'Alene mines, May announced to her family that she was going west. With that May and forty miners from Ohio set out for the Coeur d'Alenes by train. En route, May met Jim Wardner, a self-made man and founder of the town of Wardner Junction, Idaho. Wardner offered May a job as a cook in his restaurant, and she accepted. A hale and hearty May arrived in the Coeur d'Alenes, as she often said, "on the hurricane deck of a Cayuse pony," referring to her mode of travel from the banks of Lake Coeur d'Alene inland to the mining towns nestled in the hills. In reality it was the rider who would hit north Idaho like a hurricane.

Wardner's restaurant was little more than a lunch counter in a shack at the back of a saloon. Making the best of it, and with her considerable skills as a cook, May's crude cafe gained fame throughout the mining district. Before long she had opened her own restaurant and boardinghouse in Wardner Junction.

The placement of May's establishment was strategic, for when the railway came to Wardner, the tracks brought new business directly to her door. One such new customer was the train's engineer, Levi W. Hutton. A quiet, sober man, "Al" Hutton found great food and companionship at May's cafe and dined there daily. Al and May were the same age, twenty-seven, and like May, Al never really knew his parents, having been raised in an orphanage.

The couple married on November 17, 1887. May cooked all of the food for her wedding, laying out a lavish spread. Her gown was a light blue, princess-cut dress in the latest Spokane style, with pearl buttons accenting the bodice. Moments before the ceremony was to begin, the best man pulled Al aside and announced to him that he had just asked the maid of honor to marry him and would Al mind if they shared the service. The best man was also willing to pay half of the reception expenses if Al would agree to give him half of the wedding gifts. Though May coveted the spotlight, she agreed to share the wedding, but they declined the offer to divide up the wedding presents.

The newlyweds moved to Wallace, where they built a two-room cottage on the hillside near the railroad tracks. The cabin's two rooms consisted of a kitchen and a bedroom that doubled as the sitting room. Al continued to pilot his locomotive, and May ran the dining room of the Wallace Hotel. May enjoyed her newfound social status as the wife of Levi W. Hutton, but the upper echelons of Wallace society still looked down their noses at her. Large, loud, uneducated, and coarse, this woman stood out from Wallace's society wives.

When the Western Federation of Miners began to organize the miners in the Coeur d'Alene district, May made her voice heard. Since her days in the coal-mining towns of Ohio, May had been pro-labor and anti–corporate wealth. Violence between union miners and mine owners, who dismissed the union workers and replaced them with scabs, intensified.

The Huttons became personally involved in the battle on April 29, 1899, when a group of 150 miners seized Al's train at gunpoint. The miners forced Al to take the train to Gem, where they loaded forty pounds of dynamite onto a boxcar. The train took on more miners along the way until they numbered 1,000 when they reached Wardner. A gun battle ensued, but the union miners prevailed by blowing up a brand new $250,000 concentrator at the Bunker Hill and Sullivan Mine, the largest mine in the region. Two men died that day, one union and one nonunion.

Governor Steunenberg, Idaho's previously labor-friendly governor, declared Shoshone County to be in a state of insurrection and called in federal troops to maintain law and order. Up to 700 men suspected in the explosion were rounded up—including Al Hutton. The men were jailed in a hastily constructed stockade the prisoners called the Bull Pen.

May was furious at what she considered the wrongful imprisonment of her husband and what she saw as the governor's treachery. She began a ferocious letter-writing campaign to government officials and local newspapers. As another tool in her war against the mine owners, May penned a novel based on the events. She called the coroner's inquest into the deaths of the miners an "inquisition" and entitled her self-published book *The Coeur d'Alenes or a Tale of the Modern Inquisition in Idaho*. The book, which thinly veiled the identities of actual people upon which she based her characters, was a bestseller among the miners. The author sold more than 7,000 copies, mostly through labor rallies and the Western Federation of Miners.

Just a few years later, when her fortune had changed after she became a wealthy mine owner, May frantically attempted to buy back all copies of her book. She succeeded in buying back most of the books, making those that remained in private hands eventual collector's items.

Al Hutton was released from the Bull Pen after two weeks. All the other prisoners were gradually released for lack of evidence and anyone willing to testify against them. May claimed credit for their release, saying she had information that would have damaged officials if it were to have been made public. Animosity over the Bull Pen incident grew, culminating in the assassination of Governor Steunenberg by Harry Orchard, who had been hired for the job by the leaders of the Western Federation of Miners.

Orchard and his employers were tried in one of the most sensational trials of the West. They were prosecuted by senator-elect William E. Borah and were defended by Clarence Darrow. Orchard confessed to the crime, and though he testified against the union bosses, Darrow got the bosses acquitted. May Hutton became a lifelong friend of the famous attorney and earned a reputation as a force to be reckoned with for her union advocacy. Some dubbed her "The Battle-Axe of the Coeur d'Alenes," or worse.

When the Hercules began paying off for the Huttons, they moved to a large house in Wallace. Though May was now a mine owner herself, the other mine owners' wives still found her gauche, gaudy, and socially unacceptable. Short on social graces, May struggled for acceptance by entertaining prominent figures who traveled through Wallace, including Clarence Darrow; William Borah; Ella Wheeler Wilcox, a nationally acclaimed poet; Carrie

May Arkwright Hutton

Chapman Catt, a renowned suffragist; and even President Theodore Roosevelt (whom she later opposed for his statements against women's rights).

May now had the money to fully indulge her flamboyant taste in clothes. She favored styles that accentuated her bulk and drew her much attention, including a zebra-striped coat she sported. Her wild taste in hats did nothing to discourage talk among the townspeople of "that woman!"

Even though Idaho women had received the vote in 1896, May joined the National American Woman Suffrage Association and campaigned for equal suffrage throughout the West. She and Al hosted a banquet in Portland for Susan B. Anthony during the group's 1905 annual convention.

A staunch Democrat, in 1904 May decided to run for the Idaho state legislature. Her strategy was to talk to delegates individually and convince them to vote for her on their first ballot. Winning the first-ballot nomination, May then campaigned hard to be elected. Much publicity followed her campaign, and May reveled in the attention. At least one reporter referred to her as "*the* woman politician from Idaho." Although she came within eighty votes of beating her Republican opponent, May was defeated. Predictably, May blamed the loss on wealthy mine owners who funded her opponent. She also blamed the "indifference among the women voters" for her defeat.

Wanting to be closer to an investment center, Al convinced May to move to Spokane in 1907. The Hutton Block, a four-story office building that included the couple's living quarters in the penthouse, became their new home. In moving from Idaho to Washington, the politically active Mrs. Hutton lost her right to vote.

Suffrage became May's foremost cause, and she quickly rose to the position of vice president of the Washington Equal Suffrage Association. Her style and demeanor were diametrically opposed to the educated, refined president of the association, Mrs. DeVoe. Soon there was dissension among members of the association. May's background in Idaho was brought up in an exaggerated fashion as one of the Washington Equal Suffrage leaders claimed that May had been known as "Bootleg Mary" in the mining camps, that she ran a "bad house"-kept for immoral purposes—and that her language was profane and insulting. In response to one derogatory article, May wrote, "It is sufficient to me that my friends and neighbors of a quarter of a century believe in my honesty and sincerity of purpose."

After being rebuffed by the dominant suffrage movement in Washington, on October 7, 1909, May founded the Washington Political Equality League, headquartered in the Hutton Block. Further alienated by the upper-class suffragists, May claimed to be working for suffrage for "the laundry worker, the shop girl, the stenographer, the teacher, the working woman of every type, whose home and fireside and bread are earned by their own efforts." In 1910, fourteen years after their sisters in Idaho were granted suffrage, the women of Washington received the vote.

Remembering their own humble backgrounds, May and Al Hutton were constant supporters of the orphans and young mothers that "society forgot." May became personally involved in the lives of many young, unwed mothers, encouraging them to keep their children and even matching them for matrimony with lonely ranchers.

In Spokane Mrs. Hutton advocated for a juvenile court as well as for female jail matrons and separate facilities for female prisoners. She became one of the first women to serve on a jury in Spokane County when she sat as a juror in a criminal trial.

After suffrage was won for Washington women, May turned her attention increasingly to the Democratic Party. In 1912 May was elected one of the first two women ever to be sent as delegates to the Democratic Party's national convention in Baltimore. The other woman delegate was the sister of one of the party's potential nominees, Beauchamp "Champ" Clark. The press swarmed the outspoken, flamboyant delegate, and colorful stories about her flooded national newspapers, such as when an upscale Baltimore hotel objected when May hung her laundry out of her hotel window, but the strong-willed May prevailed by telling the hotel manager that she had paid for her room and she would do with it as she pleased. The exploits of Mrs. Hutton always made for good copy, and, although very supportive, her husband Al often implored, "May, don't make a spectacle of yourself."

As a delegate May carried out the wishes of the Washington delegation and voted for Champ Clark as nominee, though she deeply admired William Jennings Bryan. Former college president and governor of New Jersey, Woodrow Wilson, would be the party's nominee, later to be elected president, defeating incumbent William Taft and candidate Theodore Roosevelt. When, as secretary of state, Bryan began to advocate world peace, May took up the cause. One of her last acts was to host conventioneers to the Washington State Federation of Women's Clubs on behalf of world peace at her new home on Spokane's fashionable South Hill. Under a banner reading WOMEN FOR PEACE, women were encouraged to sign a resolution commending President Wilson for keeping the country out of the war in Europe.

May Arkwright Hutton died at her Spokane home on October 6, 1915, at the age of fifty-five. Although she had suffered from Bright's Disease (a kidney disorder) for years, the primary cause of death was listed as "degeneration of the heart." The death of this mighty force for so many causes she believed in was noted in newspapers nationwide. The *Spokane Chronicle* eulogized her as "author, suffragist, philosopher, humanitarian, and probably the best-known woman in the Northwest." Ironically, Al Hutton listed May's occupation on her death certificate simply as "housewife."

Her rise to riches in the mining towns of Idaho offered May the freedom to champion her causes. As she once wrote to her half brother in Ohio, "Now, Lyman, you just watch my smoke because I am going to do things!"

EMMA RUSSELL YEARIAN

1866–1951

The Sheep Queen of Idaho

*W*hen the train suddenly stopped in the middle of the vast prairie, the petite girl from Illinois stepped out and saw her first western sky. For the first time this young woman, who had dreamed of going west from the time she was a small child, smelled the musty-sweet aroma of sagebrush, heard the sound of a nighthawk dive, and witnessed millions of stars blanketing the night sky. It was as if she were a part of it all—part of this magnificent western prairie night that fall of 1887.

Emma Russell was born in Leavenworth, Kansas, on February 21, 1866. Her parents, William W. Russell and Della (Burbridge) Russell, moved to Illinois when Emma was a small child. William Russell, a Civil War veteran and son of a Revolutionary War veteran, was captain of the guards at Maynard Penitentiary in Illinois. At a time when most women were educated in and for the home, Emma graduated from high school in Chester, Illinois, and then from Southern Illinois Normal College at Carbondale in 1883.

In the fall of the year 1887, she said goodbye to her widowed father and set out to follow her dreams west to the Rockies. Emma arrived in the Salmon River country and found work, first as a governess and then as a teacher, following jobs from town to town until she landed at a one-room, sod-roofed schoolhouse in the Lemhi Valley. The young schoolteacher boarded with a prominent local family from whom she bought a stocky gelding, which she rode sidesaddle to and from her teaching job.

For weekend entertainment Emma traveled to dances held in various ranch houses. She played the popular tunes of the day on the piano for local partygoers. On many cold nights it was necessary to place heated rocks in the bottom of the buggy to keep the musicians' feet warm as they traveled through the cold night air. At these ranch-house dances, a fiddle player named Thomas Yearian caught the young schoolteacher's eye.

Thomas was a cattle rancher in the valley. His father had discovered gold and wisely invested the money in land rather than squandering his windfall as many miners had. Thomas Hodge Yearian and Emma Russell were married on April 15, 1889. The couple settled on the Yearians' ranch in Lemhi Canyon, on land Thomas's parents had homesteaded. While living on the homestead in a log cabin covered with a sod roof, Emma and Thomas had six children, one of whom died in childhood.

The education of her children was a top priority for Emma, and the pursuit of this goal made Emma Yearian into one of Idaho's top businesswomen, and the only woman in Idaho to run a large sheep ranch. Emma knew education cost money, and the sheep ranchers seemed to have more money than the cattle ranchers in the area. Besides, she saw much of the grassy rangeland going to waste around her. She tried to talk Thomas into giving up cattle ranching for sheep. This he refused to do, but he did agree with her plan to add sheep to the ranch. In 1908 Emma traveled to Dillon, Montana, where she introduced herself to the bank president, who also served as Montana's governor, and asked for a

IDAHO STATE HISTORICAL SOCIETY

Emma Yearian

loan to buy her first yearlings. Although he had his doubts about a woman running this business, her determination impressed the bank officer, and Emma was given her first loan. With the aid of a hired hand, her husband, and her ten-year-old son, Russell, the newly purchased 1,200 ewes were herded over the mountains and into Idaho.

Rancor left over from Idaho's Range Wars of the 1890s still festered between cattle and sheep ranchers. The Yearians' Lemhi River Valley neighbors were not pleased with Emma's new endeavor. Cattlemen hated sheep, claiming they ruined the range for cows by grazing clear to the roots, killing off all the grass. Although nobody pointed a gun at her, the neighbors did continually cause summonses to be served on Emma, ordering her to appear in court and defend her violations of the Two-Mile Limit Law. Idaho's Two-Mile Limit Law was enacted so that no sheep could be legally grazed within 2 miles of another ranch property. The narrow channel of the Lemhi Valley made it impossible to herd the sheep without crossing into the 2-mile barrier. Though she was frequently summoned to court, she was never convicted, a fact she attributed to good lawyers.

The Two-Mile Limit Law and a need for more winter grazing land prompted Emma to buy up land from neighboring ranches. By 1933 Emma Yearian's 2,500-acre ranch consisted of 5,000 head of sheep. She installed a shearing plant on the home ranch at Lemhi and a lambing camp up the canyon. Emma personally ran the operation, from hiring camp tenders and herders to dealing with the wool buyers.

People thought of the ranch as Emma's, though she ran the sheep and Thomas ran the cattle. The sheep proved more profitable. On one trip to see her out-of-state bankers, when Emma arrived by train, sitting on a coffin in the baggage car for want of available seats in the passenger car, a reporter took her picture and dubbed her "the Sheep Queen of Idaho."

In 1910 Emma built a grand, six-bedroom house of limestone block. One of its kind in the valley, the home had a generator, sixteen-volt electric lights, and indoor plumbing. To Emma's thinking this new manor was a much superior abode in which to raise her family than the sod-roofed, log cabin had been.

The Sheep Queen was an astute monitor of world affairs. Her grandson, Thomas Savage, wrote in his semibiographical novel, "Nobody touched the newspapers until she had read them; each evening after supper she retired with them to the bedroom upstairs where she had her roll top desk. . . ." She studied world events, believing they set a pattern for future trends that could well affect her business. Closely following the events unfolding in Europe in 1911, Emma believed there would soon be a war there. So, predicting the start of World War I, and knowing the soldiers would need wool uniforms, Emma asked her bankers for a loan of

$35,000 to increase her wool production in anticipation of this need. Of course her predictions were dead on, and her sheep ranch prospered through the war years.

Starting with a relatively small herd of inexpensive ewes, Emma developed one of Idaho's finest flocks of Rambouillets. She then bred Rambouillet rams with Cotswold ewes, producing fat lambs covered with abundantly thick, heavy wool—as she described them: "the best dual purpose sheep in this country."

Then came the winter of 1918. The previous summer had been unusually hot and dry, with the drought lasting well into fall. When snow hit, it hit with a vengeance. Blinding blizzards, howling winds, and below-freezing temperatures took their toll on the livestock in the valley. Hay was shipped in by train at a cost of four times the normal price. People whispered that this would be the end of the Sheep Queen. When the exorbitantly priced hay ran out, Emma got back on the train and went to see her banker, asking for a loan of $100,000. According to her grandson the banker wondered aloud why he should lend such a considerable sum of money to Emma at such a difficult time. "Because I believe in myself," was the Sheep Queen's reply. Emma Yearian returned to Lemhi with the money, which pulled the ranch through this difficult period.

Her considerable business acumen also brought the ranch through the Great Depression. During the Depression many previously successful ranchers lost everything. In her biography on Emma, Madge Yearian writes that during these years, "you could see cattle lying down dead of starvation." Emma came through, as she herself said, with "her head bloody but unbowed."

Mrs. Yearian also had her hand in many local organizations. Emma had been affiliated with the Order of the Eastern Star since 1890, and she was a member of the Episcopal Church of the Redeemer at Salmon. She was the first woman to serve on the

Lemhi County Agricultural Agency Committee; she served on the Predatory Animal Board and held both the offices of president and vice-president of the Lemhi County Wool Growers' Association. Reportedly, she presided over the Wool Growers' Association while simultaneously heading the Cattle and Horse Growers' Association. A charter member of the County Business and Professional Women's Club, she represented the group on a 1929 goodwill tour of Europe. During the tour Emma was introduced in Switzerland as a representative of the 52,000-member National Business and Professional Women's Club—and as the Sheep Queen of Idaho. A Swiss newspaper then reported that Emma was "the queen of 52,000 sheep."

In 1930 Emma ran for the Idaho State House of Representatives on the Republican ticket; Thomas was a Democrat. She became the first woman from Lemhi County to serve in the state legislature. The salary for legislators was $5.00 per day during Emma's Depression-era tenure of 1931–1932. While serving in the House, Emma was chairman of the State Library Committee and sat on the Highways, Livestock, and Mining Committees. She is credited with the passage of Idaho's brand-inspection law, which substantially curbed the practice of rustling by imposing harsh penalties for altering brands on livestock. In honor of an earlier Lemhi Valley heroine, Emma sponsored the bill that created Sacajawea Park and another bill to install a monument to the Shoshone woman on top of the Continental Divide near Salmon, Idaho. Emma's bid for reelection met with defeat, as "Hoover Democrats" came into vogue across the nation. While Thomas, the Democrat, attended the town's election-night gala, Emma quietly sat by the radio at her son's home.

Emma had a knack for storytelling and enthralled locals with her tales of early Lemhi County. She was a definitive authority on agricultural laws and property and water rights, and people sought her advice on such matters. A generous benefactor for her favorite projects and charities, Emma never turned her back on a friend or employee. The sight of Emma Yearian touring her sheep ranch on foot with the aid of a walking stick became commonplace in her later years.

The end came for eighty-five-year-old Emma on Christmas Day, 1951. A week earlier she had suffered a massive heart attack while she sat at her dining room table writing Christmas cards. The entire town of Salmon closed down for the funeral of the Sheep Queen of Idaho. In 1977 the Idaho Commission on Women's Programs elected Emma Russell Yearian to the Idaho Women's Hall of Fame in recognition of her many accomplishments.

DR. MINNIE
HOWARD
1872–1965

Pocatello's Pioneer
Physician Crusader

*A*s she picked her way through waist-high grass in the Snake River bottoms, sagebrush and brambles tugged at her long skirts, but her eyes never left the ground. The intent woman kept on spreading apart clumps of tall grass and searching the ground for signs of prior habitation. Then, a glint of reflected sunlight caught her eye. She reached for the object—a shard of broken pottery. More pottery fragments, bits of metal, artifacts, and ox shoes turned up as the searchers pawed at the dry earth. The group of historians had confirmed in their minds that this was indeed the site of Old Fort Hall.

Fort Hall, a trading post established by American trader Nathaniel Wyeth in 1834, was one of the first settlements in Idaho. The fort was sold to the Hudson's Bay Company in 1837 after the British fur company drove Wyeth out of business from their post, Fort Boise. When the fur industry declined, Fort Hall became an important stop and supply station for emigrants on the Oregon Trail. There the emigrants made the choice to go on to

Dr. Minnie Howard

California or to the Pacific Northwest. The Hudson's Bay Company occupied the fort until 1855, when Indian hostilities caused them to abandon the post.

As emigrants on the old Oregon Trail in 1852, pioneer Ezra Meeker, with his wife and son, had stopped and rested at Old Fort Hall on their way west. In 1906 a much older Meeker set out with an ox team to re-create his journey over the Oregon Trail. Meeker's purpose was to induce local people to place markers and monuments on "the famous old highway." He believed the story of the Oregon Trail was an American epic that must be preserved.

During Meeker's stop in Pocatello in 1906, he spoke to the Women's Study League. The white-bearded pioneer was shocked to find that so few people there had any knowledge of Old Fort Hall or its history. Meeker told the group that Old Fort Hall "was the most important point on any of the historic roads and trails in the United States." The words of the old pioneer captivated the secretary of the Women's Study League, Dr. Minnie Howard. This speech started a lifelong fascination with Old Fort Hall and her fight to have its historic significance recognized through the placement of an educational monument and museum at the site.

While in town, Meeker collected money from Pocatello merchants for a plaque. This money was given to the Women's Study League to carry out Meeker's request. The old pioneer was then shown the adobe bricks, the remains of the Fort Hall Stage Station, but Meeker claimed this was not the site of the original post he had visited on his way west. In the Summer of 1916, Meeker returned to Pocatello to locate the old fort. Dr. Minnie Howard knew someone who she thought could help with the search. Joe Rainey, the son of a French-Canadian trapper and an Indian mother, was working as an interpreter for the Civil Service on the Fort Hall Reservation. Joe had lived near the original fort as a young boy, before the post was destroyed by floods and the remains dismantled so that the logs could be used to construct the Fort Hall Stage Station, built 10 miles away in 1864. In the summer of 1916, Ezra Meeker returned to Pocatello to locate the old fort. Dr. Minnie Howard and her husband, Dr. W. F. Howard, introduced Meeker to Joe Rainey, and the group set out to discover the remains of the old trading post.

Though many experts disputed the group's find, the Women's Study League had a 7-foot-tall lava-shaft monument installed and dedicated by Meeker on August 27, 1921. Still the monument lacked an official plaque, and Minnie continued to fight for a bronze plaque to mark the site of Wyeth's Old Fort Hall. She spent the rest of her life gathering historical information and writing articles about the old fort. As with Dr. Minnie's Fort Hall efforts, her contributions to Idaho history and culture have had permanent effects.

Minnie Frances Hayden, the daughter of Jacob J. and Carina Jane (Wood) Hayden, was born August 23, 1872, in Memphis, Missouri. The Hayden family moved to a farm in Larned, Kansas, in 1886, and Minnie studied at Central Normal College in Great Bend, Kansas, for one year. Following this, Minnie taught school in rural Kansas sporadically from 1889 to 1898, while working to further her own education. She studied at Cook County Normal School in Englewood, Illinois; in Chicago in 1893; and at the University of Kansas in 1896.

Minnie Hayden and William Forrest Howard began their courtship around 1890 and were married in Larned, Kansas, on August 23, 1894. Both Howards continued to teach school to earn money for their education. The two worked toward their medical degrees together in Kansas City, where Minnie attended the Women's Medical College at the University of Kansas from 1897 to 1899. Her son, Dr. Richard Howard, said, "Dr. Minnie became a doctor because her husband thought she should know what a doctor's life was like. She got straight A's in medical school." After both Minnie and William Forrest graduated from medical school in 1899, they set up a joint practice in Cuba, Kansas.

Believing there was not much future in a small town like Cuba, with its population of 150, the Howards traveled west in 1900. When they stopped in Pocatello, they were introduced to James H. Brady, future Idaho governor and U.S. senator, who told them that Pocatello was "the coming community of the Northwest." The railroad town of Pocatello, with its population of 5,000 people, seemed promising to the Howards, who moved there with their first-born son in 1902.

The two doctors practiced medicine at their combination home/doctor's office located at 154 South Main Street across from Station Square. The town of Pocatello had no hospital when the Howards arrived. A drive to build a hospital in the young railroad town was started in 1903. Doctors William Forrest and Minnie Howard served on a small committee that raised money and made plans for the new hospital. The committee incorporated Pocatello General Hospital in December 1905. Once incorporated, the group sold stock, solicited donations, and secured loans for construction and operation of the new hospital. Construction began in 1906 and was finished the following year. The Pocatello General Hospital was operated by the corporation for a decade until it was purchased by the city and county in 1917. The hospital was abandoned in the mid-twentieth century when the city-county government built Bannock Memorial Hospital.

Female physicians were rarely found in the West during the early twentieth century, and Dr. Minnie was one of Idaho's first pioneer women doctors. Yet she was also a wife and mother, and Minnie raised two young sons while practicing medicine and donating her time to many civic causes. After the birth of her third son in 1908, she retired from the practice. The Howards had four sons, all of whom became physicians.

In 1904 Minnie organized the Civic Club of Pocatello. As chairman of the club committee, she secured a grant from philanthropist Andrew Carnegie to build a library for the town of Pocatello. The handsome classical building was built next to the Howard home on South Garfield in 1908. Years later it was placed on the National Register of Historic Places and became the home of the Bannock County Historical Society Museum (which was later moved to Ross Park).

With their young sons the family traveled to Austria, where they lived from 1909 to 1911, while Dr. W. Forrest Howard took surgical training. While in Europe, Minnie studied "art as a civic force" in Austria and Italy. She took her boys to weekly concerts at the Rathaus, or City Hall. When the Howards returned to Idaho, Minnie worked for an art program sponsored by the State Federation of Women's Clubs. She organized touring art exhibits and brought them to Idaho towns, large and small. Three such tours traveled to twenty-six towns in two years, accompanied by lecturers on art appreciation. Much of this private traveling cultural tour was paid for by Dr. Minnie herself.

The two-story house on South Garfield, built around 1908, was home to the Howard family for more than fifty years. Ancient Indian petroglyphs were cut from boulders, which had been found on undeveloped ground within Pocatello city limits, and incorporated into the fireplace of the new home during its construction. Dr. Minnie had tried in vain to have the city council and county commissioners preserve the boulders that contained the Indian drawings by dedicating a small natural park on the land where they stood, but when these efforts failed, she had them installed in her home to preserve them.

The interest in the Oregon Trail and Old Fort Hall, sparked by Ezra Meeker, caused Dr. Minnie to become a strong supporter and lifelong member of the Oregon Trail Memorial Association's Idaho chapter. Continuing on her historical quest, Dr. Minnie formed the Southern Idaho Historical Society in 1922 and headed the organization as its president for many years.

Minnie's writing career began in earnest when she was asked to document the history of the First Congregational Church of Pocatello. The story was published in the *Pocatello Tribune*. Over the following years the doctor wrote a series of articles about local history and, of course, Fort Hall for the *Tribune*. Studying Bannock County history whenever she could, Minnie gathered a considerable amount of information through listening to the oral histories of local pioneers. In 1931 she was appointed by the state of Idaho as the county historian for Bannock County. Another historian, G. Nicholas Ifft, wrote a flattering foreword to one of Minnie's articles: "We feel fortunate in securing a contribution for this column in the form of a 'History of Bannock County.' It is being written by Dr. Minnie F. Howard, who is probably the best-posted individual in Idaho on western history."

The town of Pocatello took its name from Shoshone Chief Pocatello, whose daughter was a friend of Dr. Minnie Howard's. Drawing on her friend's family history, Minnie wrote a feature article on the legend of Chief Pocatello's mother. The legend told of a Shoshone girl who, like Sacajawea, was captured by an enemy tribe but had managed to escape and return to her people.

Minnie cared deeply for the Indian people. Her sons remember traveling with her to the Fort Hall Reservation on Distribution Day to assist with the distribution of government commodities. Dr. Minnie often provided medical attention to the Shoshone-Bannock people. Integrating Indian speakers and music into religious services, Minnie managed an Indian Sunday at the

Congregational Church in Pocatello for many years. The service, held the last Sunday of every May, ministered to several hundred native parishioners.

A member of the Women's Christian Temperance Union, Minnie was deeply concerned about the ravages of alcohol among the Indians. As the chairman of Indian Welfare of the General Federation of Women's Clubs, she attempted to have laws enforced to keep alcohol off the reservation. Considering alcohol an unnecessary evil for all people, and being ahead of their time, Doctors William Forrest and Minnie Howard labeled alcoholism a "social disease."

During and after the First World War, a peace movement swept the country. Dr. Minnie became involved in the movement and attended the second conference on the Cause and Cure of War, sponsored by the General Federation of Women's Clubs and other national organizations. "The way to maintain peace is to prepare for peace," was the main tenet of the conference. The women's groups circulated petitions and ran newspaper advertisements calling for the peaceful resolution of many of the world's conflicts.

Dr. Minnie was a tireless crusader whose efforts helped bring a hospital to Pocatello, recognition for Old Fort Hall, cultural arts to southern Idaho, and historical awareness to Bannock County. In 1914 she was named by a local publication as "one of the most energetic, active and influential women in the state." Although she was a good wife and mother, Dr. Minnie did not find domestic duties nearly as interesting as her causes. The family lived among her piles of paper, books, files, and clutter. Minnie was not bound by traditions of the time. Her son told of one instance when "she created a sensation on a bicycle trip by wearing the garment popularized by Mrs. Bloomer. Dr. Minnie early manifested Women's Lib."

Full of energy, conversation, and a dynamic force for her causes, Dr. Minnie was active in the Southeast Idaho Historical Society, Oregon Trail Memorial Association, Department of Indian Welfare for the National Federation of Women's Clubs, National Board of Art for the Federation of Women's Clubs, Art and Travel Club, Civic Club of Pocatello, Art Study Club, Pocatello Music Club, Prohibition Party National Committee, Women's Christian Temperance Union, First Congregational Church, Order of Eastern Star, Daughters of the American Revolution, Descendants of the Mayflower Association, and the Women's Study League. She organized the City and County Social Welfare Board, was one of the first chairpersons of the Red Cross for Bannock and Caribou Counties, and was a member of the American Medical Association. As the first president of the Pocatello Women's Republican Club, she wrote the constitution for the region's first political club of women voters. "If she thought things were important, she got involved," stated her son Richard.

Forrest died in 1948, four years after the doctors celebrated their fiftieth wedding anniversary. Dr. Minnie died at the Bannock Nursing Home on September 2, 1965, at the age of ninety-three. Unfortunately, after her death, her home of more than fifty years was vandalized, and the Indian petroglyphs were dug from her fireplace and stolen. The home was later moved to a site outside of town.

As for Dr. Minnie's passionate drive to bring a monument and museum to Wyeth's Old Fort Hall, the location of the original old trading post was argued for 125 years until an archaeological excavation and analysis in 1993 confirmed that the site that Meeker and the Howards had located was indeed the old fort. The remains of the old trading post are located on private Shoshone-Bannock land on the Fort Hall Reservation and, to this day, are difficult to access. An authentic replica of Old Fort Hall was built at the top of Lava Cliffs in Ross Park by the city of Pocatello.

No official monument was ever placed at the old fort in spite of Dr. Minnie F. Howard's years of efforts. On June 25, 1983, however, Howard Mountain, northwest of Pocatello, was named after Dr. Minnie F. Howard and Dr. William Forrest Howard as an eternal tribute to their memories. At the dedication a plaque sponsored by the Bannock County Historical Society, the Business and Professional Women's Club, and Bureau of Land Management was installed on Howard Mountain. Three arrows on the plaque point to the Howard home in Pocatello, to American Falls Dam (Forrest's project), and to Old Fort Hall.

MARGARET COBB AILSHIE

1883–1959

Guardian of a Publishing Dynasty

*I*t was an unlikely place to find a Boise socialite. Far from the stylish cotillions and soirees of her Idaho home, this regal woman was now surrounded by acres of stark white crosses dotting the rich green lawn of the veteran's cemetery in France. She stood silently at one grave, quietly paying homage to the fallen young officer who would not be returning to his hometown. Like thousands of Americans in the "war to end all wars," this boy would never again see U.S. soil. The death of the serviceman from Boise had especially touched her; maybe by visiting his grave, she could bring a bit of Boise to him.

Before World War I Margaret led a charmed life. The daughter of a wealthy newspaperman, Calvin Cobb, and his wife, Fanny Lyon Cobb, she grew up surrounded by privilege. She had been born in Chicago on March 27, 1883, but had moved to Boise at the age of six. In her younger years Margaret attended Boise schools, but as a teenager, she was sent to board at Miss Porter's School in Farmington, Connecticut. She did not attend college. Returning to Boise as a young woman, she led an active social life among Boise's upper echelons. Frequent trips to Chicago and the

Margaret Cobb Ailshie

East Coast were made to attend weddings, balls, and other elite social affairs.

When the United States entered the war in Europe in 1917, women were pressed into service. Many middle-class women, previously seen only in the home or church, stepped into the workforce to replace men who had been called to battle. Other women became involved in the war effort through service in organizations such as the Red Cross.

Prior to World War I, charitable clubs for socially elite women had been mostly social affairs—places to be seen. During World War I the Red Cross was transformed into a powerful organization that met the needs of wounded soldiers and displaced refugees. When America entered the war, Red Cross volunteers turned their attention to our troops—attending to the sick, wounded, and lonely boys serving in Europe.

Margaret's mother passed away in October 1917. Perhaps because of this loss, a sense of patriotic duty, or a combination of the two, Margaret joined the Red Cross. She was first sent to New York during the great flu epidemic of 1918.

Called the Spanish Flu, many Americans believed that "Hun U Boats" (German submarines) were spreading this plague of germs in America. By mid-September of 1918, the army had suspended drafting soldiers due to the outbreak; by October panic had spread along the eastern seaboard. Saloons, theaters, poolrooms, and dance halls were closed down to avoid spreading the disease. Spitting on the sidewalk was deemed a misdemeanor, subject to a fine or imprisonment in some communities. There were not enough hospital beds to treat the sick, nor was there room in the mortuaries for all of the dead. Tents were set up to house the infected. The U.S. Surgeon General issued a call for help to the Red Cross, and 15,000 volunteers were recruited to battle the epidemic. They served in military camps, hospitals, coal fields, munitions plants, and shipyards, bringing comfort and aid to those in need.

Though the flu epidemic did not subside until spring of 1919, by late summer of 1918, Margaret found herself on a mercy ship bound for France, where she would run a canteen for U.S. soldiers. The Red Cross operated twenty-two front-line canteens in Europe, where volunteers brought a bit of home and comfort to our servicemen. The women served water, coffee, doughnuts, sandwiches, and quick meals to ambulance drivers and allied troops passing through. Always one to pitch in where she was needed, Margaret even drove an ambulance when called upon. Margaret and the other canteen workers provided refreshments and hope to wounded soldiers lying on stretchers outside makeshift hospitals. Perhaps it was on one of these stretchers that the Boise socialite met the dying officer from her hometown.

In addition to food, drink, cigarettes, and magazines, the Red Cross volunteers brought companionship and morale boosts to lonely soldiers far from home. Margaret and the canteen volunteers organized and attended dances for the servicemen, bringing them music and friendship, which might, if only temporarily, take them from the front lines to memories of home. The young soldiers Margaret befriended during her service in France kept in touch with her for years after the war, sending letters and postcards to which she personally responded.

In August of 1919 thirty-six-year-old Margaret returned to Boise to take her place by her father's side. Calvin Cobb had first visited Idaho as a cattle buyer from Chicago in 1887. An astute businessman, Cobb saw infinite possibilities in Idaho and returned two years later after purchasing a controlling interest in Idaho's premier newspaper, *The Idaho Daily Statesman*. The paper, now known as *The Idaho Statesman*, published its first edition on July 26, 1864, from a doorless, dirt-floored, log cabin in the mining town of

Boise, with its population of approximately 1,000 citizens. As William A. Goulder, a veteran editorial writer for *The Statesman*, wrote in 1910:

> Idaho and *The Statesman* began the race of life together, and they are now beginning the quarter stretch. What Idaho was in the beginning *The Statesman* was. What Idaho became from day to day *The Statesman* became. What Idaho is today is reflected in every issue and on every page, and while none of us can speak with certainty regarding the future, there are sufficient reasons upon which to found a rational opinion that the glorious future of Idaho will be shared in all its splendor with *The Idaho Statesman*.

Cobb and his partners purchased *The Statesman* from its second owner, Judge Milton Kelley, in 1889. As publisher, Cobb ran the paper for four decades. Upon the death of her brother, Lyon, in 1921, Margaret became heir apparent to *The Statesman* as Calvin Cobb's only living child. Even so, Margaret's interests continued to revolve around her social life and travel abroad.

Calvin Cobb began a vigorous campaign for civic improvements in Boise. *The Statesman* is credited with bringing the telegraph and telephone to Boise. Through the power of the press, Boise was placed on the main line of the Union Pacific Railroad. Though he was a staunch Republican in a community of Democrats, Cobb was the first employer in Idaho to contract with a labor union. "He felt that labor was not getting a fair wage," stated his daughter. This dynamic leader with his strongly worded editorials gained widespread attention nationally, even earning him a position as vice president of the Associated Press.

Perhaps due to his daughter's influence, Cobb and *The*

Statesman supported the national women's suffrage movement. Although Idaho women had been enfranchised by their state in 1896, when Margaret returned home from her World War I service, women did not have the right to vote in national elections. World War I had made women in the workforce a visible reality and forced them to be an organized presence. They would not willingly return to a powerless, voiceless position. President Woodrow Wilson summed up the situation by saying, "Unless we enfranchise women, we shall have fought to safeguard democracy which, to that extent, we have never bothered to create."

American women were granted the right to vote in 1920.

Eight years later, upon the death of her father in 1928, Margaret Cobb took the helm of *The Idaho Daily Statesman.* Margaret inherited a majority interest in the paper's stock from her father and purchased the remaining shares from her uncle, making her the sole stockholder. Readily admitting that she knew nothing of running a newspaper, Margaret at first relied heavily on *The Statesman's* manager. She proved to be a quick study, rapidly learning the ropes of the newspaper-publishing business.

In 1929, a year after becoming the publisher of *The Statesman,* Margaret married James F. Ailshie Jr., becoming known in the newsroom as Mrs. "A." Ailshie was the son of Idaho's Supreme Court Justice James F. Ailshie, and a prominent attorney himself. The marriage was a short and unhappy union, ending in divorce. James passed away in 1938.

Although it was her desire to continue her father's publishing legacy exactly as he had conducted it, Margaret engineered the paper's greatest progress during her regime as publisher. Under her direction *The Statesman* began publishing the paper's evening edition. Nine days later she purchased the rival *Boise Capital News* and merged it into her evening edition of *The Statesman.* Several small-town papers, such as *The Twin Falls Telegram,* were also added to *The Statesman's* holdings. As publisher, Mrs. "A" set a goal of obtaining circulation of 30,000 papers for the daily edition and 40,000 for the Sunday edition. This goal was met and exceeded when the Sunday edition reached a circulation of 50,000 during her reign as publisher.

Mrs. "A" was continually promoting new ideas. *The Statesman* became one of the premier newspapers in the Northwest, subscribing to four national wire services and purchasing the columns of most of the nation's best-known editorialists—Mrs. "A" declined, however, to publish Eleanor Roosevelt's column, saying, "She does not write well enough."

Calvin Cobb had constructed the building that had housed *The Statesman* from 1910 to 1950 in the style of the brick buildings found in old Philadelphia, complete with window boxes and handwrought ironwork. When the time came for *The Statesman* to expand its headquarters, Margaret sought a design of modern architecture. A nationally prominent architect was hired to design the two-story marble structure. Several possible sites were studied for the new building. Margaret chose an attractive and practical location on Sixth and Bannock, facing Steunenberg Park and surrounded by Boise City Hall, the Idaho State Capitol, and federal buildings.

After the move to the new location in 1952, Margaret continued to purchase modern equipment and install new machinery in order to bring *The Statesman* to the level she believed would sustain the paper through Boise's continued expansion.

Margaret Ailshie, who had resided in the Cobb family mansion in Boise for all but the first six years of her life, was devoted to the city. She supported many civic enterprises and contributed to numerous Boise charitable, religious, and educational organizations. Cultural activities in the city were promoted by the paper and its publisher, an enthusiastic patron of the arts.

Mrs. "A" not only financially supported but often personally attended the annual Basque Ball held during the Christmas season. During the event the Boise Basques held a sheep auction to benefit charity. Margaret was a generous bidder.

The Statesman brought the United States Marine Corps Band to Boise to perform for the city. In addition to sponsoring the concerts, the paper transported thousands of high-school music students from southern Idaho and eastern Oregon to attend a matinee performance of the noted band.

Margaret was the driving force behind the construction of Bronco Stadium at Boise Junior College, now Boise State University. *The Idaho Statesman,* under Margaret's direction, advanced almost the entire cost of building the stadium. She believed that Boise needed a structure that could seat a crowd of 10,000. Bronco Stadium was built to accommodate 10,800. (The original wooden stadium has since been replaced by one that seats 30,000.)

Another of Margaret's pet projects was the restoration of pioneer cabins and early vehicles on display as part of Julia Davis Park. The city of Boise had accepted land from the wealthy Davis family in 1907, naming the park in honor of the benefactor's wife, Julia Davis, who had died that same year. Margaret planned and supervised the restoration of log cabins and rustic vehicles and the construction of buildings to house the early pioneer conveyances and display them to the public.

Margaret gave many years of service to the Boise Park Board and Boise chapters of the Salvation Army and the Red Cross. During World War II Mrs. "A" flew to England as a guest of the *British Press,* to examine conditions among American troops. In the final years of her life, Margaret incorporated the Margaret Cobb Ailshie Trust, with the hope of creating a perpetual source of funding for Boise charities and educational institutions.

The publicity-shy Margaret did not enjoy seeing her own name in print. Though she had been the subject of articles in both *Time* magazine and the New York *Daily News,* her own staff knew to delete her name when it appeared in copy.

Although she had the same aristocratic bearing as her father, Margaret was accessible and a great friend to those who worked for her at *The Statesman.* She knew most of her newspaper employees and their families personally and considered their welfare a top priority. Members of her staff often described her as "gracious, generous, and easy to work for." As publisher, Mrs. "A" commanded the respect of all who had business dealings with her "Whether one is a friend or an enemy, he can't help according her respect. Only a singularly intelligent and energetic person could take over a project as a complete greenhorn and make a success out of it as Mrs. "A" has done with *The Statesman,*" noted one anonymous Boisean.

In the last few years of her life, Margaret lost her eyesight and became an invalid suffering from chronic malnutrition. She passed away on August 26, 1959, at the age of seventy-six. With Margaret's death the Cobb family's seventy-year legacy of publishing *The Idaho Statesman* came to an end. The reins of the paper were passed to the general manager, James L. Brown. Brown, who had managed the paper under Margaret for nearly twenty years, commented on the impact she had had on *The Statesman:*

> All of us at *The Statesman* have realized for some time that Mrs. Ailshie's health had been failing and that her frail body, racked by chronic malnutrition of years' standing, would not much longer be able to withstand the developing complications. Yet her death is an enormous shock to every one of us who knew her and

had the benefit of her kindness, her liberality and her great personality. She was scrupulously honest. As a newspaper publisher she was fearless. She insisted that *The Statesman* conduct a vigorous editorial policy. She abhorred what she called a "dull" newspaper. It is difficult to realize that she no longer will guide the destiny of *The Statesman* newspapers. It is not possible at this immediate time to consider the future without her counsel and friendliness.

The Statesman, as an independently owned newspaper, did not survive Margaret by many years. Four years after her death, Brown sold the paper to Federated Publications of Michigan. Federated Publications later merged with the paper's current owners, Gannett Company.

The first annual distribution of funds by the Margaret Cobb Ailshie Trust was made in 1961, providing $25,000 to Idaho hospitals, convalescent homes, orphanages, colleges, and, of course, the Boise chapter of the American Red Cross. Two years later, in a fitting tribute, James L. Brown purchased the red-brick building that had housed *The Idaho Statesman* from 1910 to 1952 and donated it to the Red Cross in memory of Margaret Cobb Ailshie.

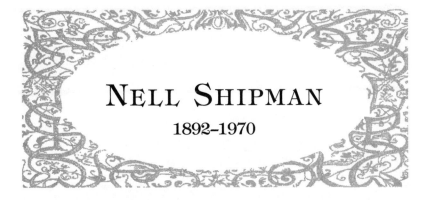

NELL SHIPMAN
1892–1970

The Girl from God's Country

*D*elirious with pain and fever, Bert set out across the frozen lake in a dogsled before the break of day. Unable to stop her lover, Nell strapped a pair of snowshoes to her feet and chased after the sled. Two feet of slushy snow covered the treacherous ice, which she could hear cracking under her weight. When the sled hit an impasse, Bert had not the wits to get around it, and Nell caught up with him and loaded him onto the dogsled. The woman mustered all of her strength to lift the sled and dogs over natural barriers. Several times Nell went into the freezing lake water up to her hips in order to guide the sled along.

For the next 2 miles, the pair made good time, until they encountered open water. Then Nell guided the dogs over a narrow rim of ice along the shoreline. When they could no longer follow the shoreline, the pair broke trail through 5 feet of snow onshore. Nell removed her soaking-wet socks, knowing that if they froze to her feet, she would get frostbite.

When it seemed they could go no farther, a neighbor and his brother caught up to the two. Dragging a boat on a sled over the ice until they hit navigable water, and finishing the last 3 miles on

Nell Shipman

foot, the foursome finally arrived in Coolin. The couple traveled to Spokane from Priest River by train, where their story made national headlines. "Win Desperate Struggle For Life In Snow and Cold of North Idaho," was the front-page headline in the January 19, 1924 *Spokesman-Review*. The article began:

> Facing death hourly for two intolerable days, living through periods when they almost welcomed death to relieve their suffering, Nell Shipman, moving picture star, and Bert Van Tuyle, her husband [sic] and director, beat their way through 30 miles of snow and cold and water in one of the most desperate struggles through which it is possible for human beings to live.

Silent-screen star Nell Shipman could not have created a more dramatic scene for one of her movies as that which she endured in real life. While filming one of Nell's movies, *Back to God's Country*, Van Tuyle had suffered severe frostbite to his right foot. Left untreated, the foot troubled Bert for years and eventually became infected with gangrene, which progressed to blood poisoning and fever. Stranded at their home on northern Priest Lake, which was accessible only by boat in summer and dogsled in winter, Bert, in his delirium, set out on his own to get medical attention. Bert's toes were amputated when he finally reached the hospital in Spokane.

In a 1987 article for The *Spokesman-Review*, Susan English wrote:

> A silent movie shot on the Canadian tundra in 1919 made actress Nell Shipman a household name in the 1920s. Living through three harsh winters on the north shores of remote Priest Lake with a film crew, her lover and a menagerie of more than 100 animals made her a legend.

The talented actress, writer, director, and producer broke ground in the silent-movie industry as a woman in a male-dominated business. Her movie characters were not the helpless, weak, female victims seen in most silent movies. Rather, Nell portrayed strong, intelligent, free-willed women who always outwitted the villains.

It was not only her sex that set Nell Shipman apart from other moviemakers of the time; most silent movies were shot on Hollywood sets, but Nell insisted on reality and filmed her movies on location—one of the first directors to do so. The same sense of realism led Nell to her first nude scene. Nell was slated to wear a flesh-colored suit in a simulated nude scene, but she did not like the look of the wet fabric draping off her body. On her own volition she shed the suit and performed the scene *au naturel.* *Back to God's Country* became only the second silent picture filmed in America to feature a nude scene.

An advocate of animal rights, Nell kept her own zoo of animal characters and treated them humanely while filming. This approach to animals was foreign in an era when trip wires, whips, and electric-shock treatments were used industry-wide. Through her series of North Woods adventure films featuring animal actors, Nell became famous as *The Girl From God's Country*, the title of one of her films.

Nell Shipman was born Helen Foster-Barham on October 25, 1892, in Victoria, British Columbia, the second child of British immigrants to Canada. When young Helen was ten years old, Arnold and Rose Barham moved their family to Seattle, where Helen was bitten by the acting bug. She was just thirteen when she began touring with an acting company. On the road the young actress played the piano, danced, and sang, and by 1909, she was the lead in a stock-company production that toured Alaska, British Columbia, Idaho, Utah, and Washington. Rose Barham joined her daughter on vaudeville tours as a chaperon, costume maker, and general caretaker.

By the age of eighteen, Helen Barham had starred as a leading lady in stock productions, repertory theater, and vaudeville and had toured in a road show. On her eighteenth birthday, while seeking work at Seattle's Third Avenue Theater, she met Ernest Shipman, the stock company's manager. In 1911 the young actress became the fourth wife of future film producer and promoter Ernie Shipman. During the first few years of the marriage, Helen acted in Shipman's plays and wrote and starred in her first movie, *The Ball of Yarn*. Early in her film career, Helen took her nickname, Nell, as her stage name.

The couple's son, Barry, was born February 24, 1912, at the Shipman's new home in Pasadena, California. During her pregnancy, when she could not act, Nell wrote screenplays for movies. She sold the rights to her screenplay called *Under the Crescent* to Universal Studios and was paid $1,000 by Grosset & Dunlap to turn the script into a novel. Nell's reputation in Hollywood as a talented writer, actress, and director was growing. The 1916 film *God's Country and the Woman*, which Nell acted in, directed, and produced, made her a movie star.

Disdaining Hollywood's image of a leading lady, Nell turned down a seven-year contract with Goldwyn Studios, saying:

> I was summoned to the office of Mr. Goldfish, not yet turned Goldwyn, and offered a seven-year contract. . . But I did not like the way they dressed their contract players. This was in the period of curly blondes with Cupid's-bow mouths; and Wardrobe's main idea was to bind down a bosom with a swatch of shiny material which met yards of floaty gauze at the waistline and looked like a flower penwiper.

Instead, Nell made a series of movies based on novels by adventure writer James Oliver Curwood. Ironically, by the time *Back to God's Country* (shot in the Canadian north in 1919) had made Nell Shipman a household name, her relationships with Curwood and with her producer, husband Ernest, had been dissolved.

Race-car driver Bert Van Tuyle was Nell's next love interest, and she made him production manager, codirector, and partner in her new movie-production company, Nell Shipman Productions. It was during the filming of *Back to God's Country* that Van Tuyle—standing in for the film's leading man, who had died of pneumonia—suffered the frostbite that would lead to the partial amputation of his foot.

After filming *The Girl from God's Country* in 1921, Van Tuyle and Shipman took their next joint production, *The Grub Stake*, to Minnehaha Studios in Spokane. "One day a very attractive lady visited the studio. She had an abundance of dark brown hair and beautiful brown eyes. She had a vivacious smile that really made you sit up and take notice," wrote Lloyd Peters, who was hired onto Nell's crew. Peters described the filming of *The Grub Stake*:

> We worked all night filming scenes in the rain . . . you should have seen us by morning! Poor Nell! In one scene she was fleeing from the villain, trying to escape up a steep path with the rain blowing in her face. She ended up crawling in the mud on her hands and knees. It made a wonderful picture, but by morning she looked like a half drowned mud hen.

Bent on filming the outdoor sequences on location, Nell moved her animals and crew to Priest Lake, Idaho, in August of 1922, to complete *The Grub Stake*. Nell thought Priest Lake the perfect location for a series of films based on the great North Woods. Her love for Priest Lake lasted throughout her lifetime, as she recorded in her autobiography: "Did you ever come to a place and instantly recognize it as your Ultima Thule [ultimate northernmost place], the one spot in all God's world where you belonged? . . . Such a spot, so it seemed to me, was Priest Lake, in Idaho."

Lionhead Lodge was built in the winter of 1922, on the northeastern shore of Priest Lake—an area more than 20 miles from the nearest road, 50 miles from the railroad, and accessible only by boat in summer and snowshoe or dogsled in winter. Asked why she needed such an out-of-the-way location, Nell told her board of directors, "I want exteriors to match the true locale of the story I am filming, and to me Priest Lake is the loveliest, wildest, most perfect spot of all." Nearly one hundred animals, including bears, raccoons, timber wolves, elk, deer, skunks, badgers, porcupines, beavers, foxes, coyotes, lynx, bobcats, cougars, horses, and eagles, were barged up the lake.

While in Hollywood, Nell had been sickened by the cruelty used to get animals to perform in the movies. In her autobiography she wrote of seeing a bobcat prodded with electric shocks to make it hop and snarl, then given drugs to make it still, the combination of which killed the animal:

> I cried over the limp furpiece. . . . Then my determination to do something for their cause was born. I knew it would be a small beginning; but, if I could show these animals on the screen doing their stuff freely, uncaged, unafraid, then a step would be taken, a smidgen of communication established between fellow creatures.

Nell then decided to assemble her own wild-animal cast and "make actors of them without the use of whips, shouted commands, [or] charged wires poked into them."

At Lionhead Lodge the production company worked hard. Nell and her crew brought all supplies and materials in via boat or dogsled. They built their own cabins and cages for more than seventy wild animals and two dogsled teams. Life at Lionhead included chopping wood, fishing, hunting, and caring for Nell's zoo. Lloyd Peters, a member of Nell's crew and author of *Lionhead Lodge*, remembered:

> Everyone did a little bit of everything, and everyone, including Nell, did their part! We cared for the animals, fed them, cleaned the pens, built scenery and freighted our supplies by dog sled in winter, cut wood, shot outdoor scenes from here to the top of Lookout Mountain. I would do it all over again if I had the chance.

Lionhead Lodge was home, office, and movie set for Nell, Van Tuyle, and her crew. Nell loved the area and repaid the community by organizing a benefit performance to raise money to outfit the Priest River town band with uniforms. In appreciation the band serenaded Nell whenever she was a guest at the Hotel Charbonneau in Priest River.

Following *The Grub Stake*, two movies were shot on location at Priest Lake: *Trail of the Northwind* and *The Light on Lookout*. For *The Light on Lookout*, the crew had to transport their cameras and equipment 6,724 feet up Lookout Mountain. While on production in Idaho between 1922 and 1924, Nell Shipman Productions also filmed *White Water*, *Wolf's Brush*, and *The Love Tree*. She called the series of movies The Little Dramas of the Big Places.

A stickler for realism, Nell sent her young son, Barry, into the frigid lake repeatedly for multiple takes during the filming of one winter scene. She then held Barry underwater by the shirt to prevent him from climbing out of the freezing lake water too fast while the cameras were rolling.

Filming on Priest Lake for almost three years took a toll on Nell's production company and her relationship with Bert. Finding financing for her films became increasingly difficult. Independent filmmakers were being squeezed out of business by the movie conglomerates, and crews came and went from the remote movie sets.

On Christmas Day, 1924, when Nell took up with a handsome actor, Van Tuyle threatened to shoot her. At that, Nell ran from the cabin onto the ice-covered lake, intending to throw herself into the water. Her twelve-year-old son had to physically restrain her from harming herself. Barry and Nell went to Spokane the following day to restore Nell's mental state. She never returned to Lionhead Lodge.

Lionhead Lodge had fallen on hard times, and Nell could not afford to feed her animals. With her Nell Shipman Productions deeply in debt, creditors took ownership of the animals. In 1925 stories circulated across the country that Nell Shipman's animals were starving in their cages at Priest Lake. Some of the animals did not survive the harsh, north Idaho winters, and those remaining were sold to the San Diego Zoo. Nell claimed that bad publicity about the treatment of the animals made it difficult for her to obtain financing for her next movies.

Nell married actor Charles Ayers in 1925. The couple moved to Spain on a yearlong honeymoon, where Nell convinced Charles to change his name to the more-romantic-sounding Carlos de Corveda. Twins, Charles and Daphne, were born to the couple on May 3, 1926, in Spain. Charles and Nell divorced in 1934, and she took up with her last great love, Baron Amerigo Serrao—aka Peter Locke. That relationship, described by Barry Shipman as "a case of a Dreamer being nourished by another Dreamer," ended four years after it began.

When "talkies" were introduced, Nell attempted to recapture her movie-star status but was unsuccessful. She did achieve success as a writer with a number of screenplays, movie scripts, magazine articles, and two novels. Perhaps her best-known screenplay was the script for the film *Wings in the Dark*, starring Cary Grant and Myrna Loy. While living in Cabazon, California, Nell wrote her autobiography, *The Silent Screen and My Talking Heart*, which was published in 1969. On January 23, 1970, a year after she had completed the manuscript for her book, Nell Shipman passed away. Originally, Nell had intended her autobiography to be a three-book series, but the last two were never written.

In 1971 Canada named Nell "the First Lady of Canadian Cinema." On August 31, 1977, the state of Idaho honored Nell Shipman when they named the site of the former Lionhead Lodge "Nell Shipman Point." The point of land commemorating Nell is located in the Lionhead Park Camp Ground unit of Priest Lake State Park, between Mosquito Bay and Lion Creek. In his dedication Idaho's Lieutenant Governor William J. Murphy recognized Nell's contributions to the state of Idaho, proclaiming:

> "Shipman Point" will forever be a constant memorial to the courageous woman whom we honor today. . . . The vision that Nell Shipman had in filming in what has been described as "The Showland of the Northwest" is now reoccurring as feature film and television production companies are beginning to appraise Idaho as a veritable goldmine of possible set locations. Today, a more realistic, sophisticated audience has demanded

realism in scenery and background; a realism in which Nell Shipman's films portrayed from the very first. . . . To the relatives of Nell Shipman I thank you for the honor which is brought to Idaho.

Other than her highly successful *Back to God's Country*, there were no known copies of Nell's movies in existence until 1985, when Boise State University initiated a worldwide search for the films. By 1987 Boise State University's Hemingway Western Studies Center had amassed a collection of six of Nell Shipman's motion pictures. Claiming they had the most complete collection of Nell Shipman's movies in the entire world in their All-Idaho Film Collection, Boise State University sponsored a Nell Shipman Silent Film Festival in the spring of 1987.

Nell Shipman's work is being rediscovered and appreciated today for its relevance to modern issues. She is hailed as a true woman of foresight and courage and a genuine movie pioneer.

BIBLIOGRAPHY

MARGARET COBB AILSHIE

Austin, Judith. "Margaret Cobb Ailshie." *Idaho State Historical Society Reference Series* (1971): No. 734.

Beal, Merrill D., Ph.D., and Merle W. Wells, Ph.D. *History of Idaho*. Vol. III. New York: Lewis Historical Publishing Company, Inc., 1959.

Calvin Cobb—Obituaries. Newspaper clippings—biographical files. Idaho State Historical Society, 8–10 November 1928.

d'Easum, Dick. "Through These Mellow Pages March the Legions of History." *The Idaho Statesman*, 26 July 1964.

Defenbach, Byron. *IDAHO The Place and Its People*. Chicago/New York: The American Historical Society, Inc., 1933.

"Margaret Cobb Ailshie: Guardian of the Policy." *The Idaho Statesman*, 26 July 1964.

"Margaret Cobb Ailshie, Statesman Publisher, Dies." *The Idaho Statesman*, 27 August 1959.

"Margaret Cobb Ailshie Trust Board Announces First Fund Distribution." *The Idaho Statesman*, 6 May, 1962.

"Red Cross Involvement in the First World War (1914–1919)." American Red Cross–Virtual Museum. The American National Red Cross, 2000. On-line. www.redcross.org

Rhea, Rt. Rev. Frank A. "Eulogy for Mrs. Ailshie." Funeral Eulogy, August 1959.

Smith, Olevia. *Idaho's First Lady of The Press*. Unpublished manuscript. Moscow, Ida.: Special Collections University of Idaho Library, 1946.

POLLY BEMIS

Abrams, Joan. "Myths of Polly." *Lewiston Morning Tribune*, 10 January 1997.

Bailey, Robert G. *River of No Return.* Lewiston, Ida. R.G. Bailey Printing Company, 1935

Bancroft, George. "China Polly—A Reminiscence." Unpublished manuscript. Boise: Idaho State Historical Society, not dated.

"Czizek Explodes Myth of Chinese Poker Bride." *The Idaho Statesman,* 24 September 1933.

Elsensohn, Sister M. Alfreda. *Idaho County's Most Romantic Character: Polly Bemis.* Caldwell, Ida.: The Caxton Printers, Ltd, 1978/Cottonwood, Ida. Idaho Corporation of Benedictine Sisters, 1987.

————. "Memories of Polly Bemis." *The Spokesman-Review,* 12 May 1957.

————. "Polly Bemis Memoirs Included In Academy's Historical Display." *Lewiston Tribune,* 18 May 1957.

d' Easum, Dick. "She Won Her Man With a Crochet Hook." *The Idaho Statesman,* 27 October 1957.

Gizycka, Countess Eleanor Patterson. "Diary on The Salmon River." *Field and Stream,* June (1923). Reprinted *Idaho Yesterdays,* Spring (1997): Vol. 41, No. 1.

Johnson, Lamont. "Old China Woman of Idaho Famous." *The Sunday Oregonian,* 5 November 1933.

"Polly Bemis, 'Poker Bride' Of Salmon River Country, Expires." *Lewiston Tribune,* 7 November 1933.

Swinney, H.J. "Polly Bemis 'Poker Bride,' Recalled As Impact of Chinese Upon Gem State Review." *The Idaho Statesman,* 26 December 1957.

"Twenty Years Ago—In The Statesman." *The Idaho Statesman,* 8 August 1954.

Wegars, Priscilla, Ph.D. "My Search For The 'Real' Polly Bemis." *Idaho Humanities,* Summer (1998): 1, 4, 8.

————. "Polly Bemis." *Asian American Comparative Collection: Ongoing Research.* Moscow, Ida.: Laboratory of Anthropology, University of Idaho, January 1999.

Zaunmiller, Frances. "Polly Bemis, Part of Salmon River History." *Idaho County Free Press*, 16 June 1966: Vol. 79, No. 49.

DR. MINNIE HOWARD

Beal, Merrill D., Ph.D., and Merle W. Wells, Ph.D. *History of Idaho*. Vol II. New York: Lewis Historical Publishing Company, Inc., 1959.

"Dr. Minnie Howard, Early Leader, Dies." *Idaho State Journal*, 3 September 1965.

Hart, Arthur. "Minnie F. Howard: Physician, Mother, Patron of the Arts." *The Idaho Statesman*, 21 May 1979.

Kennedy, Mary Virginia. *A Study of Dr. Minnie F. Howard*. Unpublished manuscript. Denver, Colo.: University of Denver, April 1968.

Kissane, Dr. Leedice. "Howard Family." *The Idaho Statesman*, 18 July 1982

———. "Dr. Richard Howard Recalls His Boyhood." *The Idaho Statesman*, 25 July 1982.

———. "Dr. Minnie Had Interest in Local History." *The Idaho Statesman*, 1 August 1982.

Meeker, Ezra. *Ox-Team Days on the Oregon Trail*. Yonkers-on-Hudson, N.Y.: World Book Company, 1922.

"Plaque Confirms Role of Pioneers." *Idaho State Journal*, 16 October 1983.

Ruckman, JoAnn, Ph.D., and Sylvia Cline. "Minnie F. Howard." *Biographical Sketches*. Idaho State University, Eli M. Oboler Library, 17 June 1998. On-line. www.isu.edu/library/special/mc001b.htm.

Wischmann, Lesley. "Fort Hall." *Virtual Tour of the Oregon Trail*. Independence, Mo.: Oregon-California Trails Association, 1998. On-line. www.OCTA-trails.org.

MAY ARKWRIGHT HUTTON

Bean, Margaret. "She Was A Woman Who Spoke Her Mind." *The Spokesman-Review*, 12 July 1936.

Fargo, Lucile F. *Mrs. Hercules*. Unpublished manuscript. Spokane: Northwest Room, Spokane Public Library, undated.

———. *Spokane Story*. New York: Columbia University Press, 1950.

Horner, Patricia Voeller. "May Arkwright Hutton: Suffragist and Politician." In *Women in Pacific Northwest History*. Edited by Karen Blair. Seattle: University of Washington Press, 1988.

Hutton, May Arkwright. *The Coeur d'Alenes or A Tale of the Modern Inquisition in Idaho*. Fairfield, Wash.: Ye Galleon Press, 1985. First published, Wallace, Ida./Denver: Self-published/May Arkwright Hutton, 1900

————. Scrapbooks, clippings from unidentified newspapers, Spokane: Eastern Washington State Historical Society, undated.

Kizer, Benjamin H. "May Arkwright Hutton." *Pacific Northwest Quarterly*, April (1966): Vol. 57, No. 2.

Montgomery, James W. *Liberated Woman*. Fairfield, Wash.: Ye Galleon Press, 1985.

JO MONAGHAN

Adams, Mildretta. *Historic Silver City: The Story of the Owyhees*. Homedale, Ida.: Owyhee Chronicle, 1960.

"Cowboy Jo—Was a Woman!" *American-Journal-Examiner*, March 1904.

"Desperate Women: 'Little Jo' Monoghan." *New York Post*, Sunday, 21 December 1952.

"Fifty Years Ago." *The Idaho Statesman*, 24 January 1954.

"Joe Monaghan's Life." *The Idaho Daily Statesman*, 13 January 1904.

"Joe Monaghan Was a Woman." *The Idaho Daily Statesman*, 12 January 1904.

"'Joe' Monnaghan." *Idaho Capital News*, 28 January 1904.

"Local." *Owyhee Avalanche*, 15 January 1904.

Penson, Betty. "Death Ended Cowboy's Masquerade." *The Idaho Statesman*, 17 December 1978.

————. "Little Joe, Idaho Cowboy With a Secret." *The Idaho Statesman*, 4 February 1979.

Rickert, Roger. "Little Jo." *Frontier Times*, June–July (1971): 39, 52–53.

"Was She a Bender." *Lewiston Morning Tribune*, 8 March 1904.

SACAJAWEA

Anderson, Irving W. "Sacajawea?—Sakakawea?—Sacagawea?" *We Proceeded On,* Summer (1975). Reprinted by The Lewis & Clark Trail Heritage Foundation. On-line. www.lewisandclark.org.

Beal, Merrill D., Ph.D. and Merle W. Wells, Ph.D. *History of Idaho.* Vol II. New York: Lewis Historical Publishing Company, Inc., 1959.

Bergon, Frank. *The Journals of Lewis and Clark.* New York: Viking Penguin, Inc., 1989.

Clarke, Charles G. *The Men of the Lewis and Clark Expedition.* Glendale, Calif.: The Arthur H. Clark Company, 1970.

Defenbach, Byron. *Red Heroines of the Northwest.* Caldwell, Ida.: The Caxton Printers, Ltd., 1935.

Flandrau, Grace. *A Glance at the Lewis and Clark Expedition.* Great Northern Railway, 1927.

Hebard, Grace Raymond. *Sacajawea, a Guide and Interpreter of the Lewis and Clark Expedition.* Glendale, Calif.: The Arthur H. Clark Company, 1933.

Howard, Harold P. *Sacajawea.* Norman: University of Oklahoma Press, 1971.

Rees, John E. "The Shoshoni Contribution to Lewis and Clark." *Idaho Yesterdays,* Summer (1958): Vol. II, No. 2.

Thwaites, Reuben Gold. *Original Journals of the Lewis & Clark Expedition, 1804–1806.* New York: Dodd, Mead & Co., 1904.

NELL SHIPMAN

Armatage, Kay. "The Silent Scream and My Talking Heart." *About Nell Shipman.* Toronto, Canada: University of Toronto, 12 December 1997. On-line, Bishay, J. www.utoronto.ca/shipman.

Bankson, Russell Arden. "Win Desperate Struggle For Life In Snow and Cold of North Idaho." *Spokane Daily Chronicle,* 19 January 1924.

Brownlow, Kevin. *The Parade's Gone By.* New York: Alfred A. Knopf, 1967.

"Crowds Pack Theater To See 'The Grubstake.'" *Spokane Chronicle*, 24 February 1923.

English, Susan. "Nell." *The Spokesman-Review, Spokane Chronicle*, 22 February 1987.

Foster, Gwendolyn. *Women Film Directors: An International Bio-Critical Dictionary*. Conn.: Greenwood Press, 1995.

"Idaho to Honor Nell Shipman." *Priest River Times*, 14 July 1977.

"Idaho's Salute To An Actress." *Scenic Idaho* (1977): Vol. 30, No.3.

"Movie Menagerie Near Starvation." *The Spokesman-Review*, 9 June 1925

"Nell Shipman Now Novelist." *The Spokesman-Review*, 22 May 1930.

Peters, Lloyd. *Lionhead Lodge*. Fairfield, Wash.: Ye Galleon Press, 1976.

Shipman, Nell. *The Silent Screen and My Talking Heart*. Boise, Ida.: Hemingway Western Studies Series, Boise State University Press, 1987.

Simpson, Claude. "Aug. 31 Dedication For Shipman Point." *Priest River Times*, 25 August 1977.

———. "More On Nell Shipman Silent Screen Pioneer." *Priest River Times*, 21 July 1977.

———. "More on Silent Film Pioneer, Nell Shipman." *Priest River Times*, 11 August 1977.

———. "Nell Shipman Point." *Incredible Idaho*. Spring (1978): Vol. 9, No. 4.

JANE TIMOTHY SILCOTT

Bailey, Robert G. *River of No Return*. Lewiston, Ida.: R.G. Bailey Printing Company, 1935.

Defenbach, Byron. *Red Heroines of the Northwest*. Caldwell, Ida.: The Caxton Printers, Ltd., 1935.

Drury, Clifford Merrill. *Henry Harmon Spalding*. Caldwell, Ida.: The Caxton Printers, Ltd., 1936.

————. *Where Wagons Could Go*. Lincoln, Nebr.: University of Nebraska Press/Bison Books, 1997. First published as *First White Women Over the Rockies*. Vol I. Glendale, Calif.: Arthur H. Clark & Co., 1963.

Evans, Pauline. *The Old Spalding Log Cabin Mission, and the Story of Princess Jane*. Unpublished manuscript. Pullman, Wash.: Washington State University Libraries, 26 November 1935.

LOUISE SIUWHEEM

Bradley, Rt. Rev. Cyprian, O.S.B. and Most Rev. Edward J. Kelly, D.D., Ph.D. *History of the Diocese of Boise 1863–1952*. Boise: Roman Catholic Diocese of Boise, Caldwell: The Caxton Printers, Ltd., 1953.

Chittenden, Hiram Martin and Alfred Talbot Richardson. *Life, Letters and Travels of Father Pierre-Jean De Smet, S.J. 1801–1873*. New York: Francis P. Harper, 1905.

De Smet, Rev. P. J., S. J. *New Indian Sketches*. New York: D. & J. Sadlier & Co., 1865.

Dozier, Jack. "The Light of the Coeur d'Alenes." *The Spokesman-Review*, 15 July 1962.

Hultner, Vi. "The Good Grandmother of the Coeur d'Alenes." *The Spokesman-Review*, 7 December 1952.

Hutton, May Arkwright. *The Coeur d'Alenes or A Tale of the Modern Inquisition in Idaho*. Fairfield, Wash.: Ye Galleon Press, 1985. First published, Wallace, Ida./Denver: Self-published/May Arkwright Hutton, 1900.

LaVeille, E., S. J. *The Life of Father De Smet, S. J.* New York: P. J. Kenedy & Sons, 1915.

Point, Rev. Nicolas, S. J. *Biographies of the Coeur d'Alene*. Unpublished manuscript. DeSmet, Ida.: Sacred Heart Mission, circa 1892.

ELIZA HART SPALDING/ELIZA SPALDING WARREN

Dawson, Deborah Lynn. *Laboring in My Savior's Vineyard: The Mission of Eliza Hart Spalding*. Unpublished dissertation. Ann Arbor, Mich.: University Microfilms, 1988/Boise, Ida.: Idaho State Historical Society Microfilms, 1988.

Drury, Clifford Merrill. *Henry Harmon Spalding*. Caldwell, Ida.: The Caxton Printers, Ltd., 1936.

———. *Where Wagons Could Go*. Lincoln, Nebr.: University of Nebraska Press/Bison Books, 1997. First published as *First White Women Over the Rockies*. Vol I. Glendale, Calif.: Arthur H. Clark Co., 1963.

Gray, William H. *A History of Oregon*. Published by the author for subscribers. Portland: Harris & Holman, San Francisco: H. H. Bancroft & Co. New York: The American News Company, 1870.

Meany, Edmond S. "Living Pioneers of Washington." *The Post-Intelligencer*, 1 December 1915.

Nixon, Oliver W. *How Marcus Whitman Saved Oregon*. Chicago: Star Publishing Company, 1895.

Sager, Catherine, Elizabeth Sager and Matilda Sager. *The Whitman Massacre of 1847*. Fairfield, Wash.: Ye Galleon Press, 1986.

Warren, Eliza Spalding. *Memoirs of the West: The Spaldings*. Portland, OR: Marsh Printing Company, 1916.

Whitman, Narcissa. *The Letters of Narcissa Whitman*. Fairfield, Wash.: Ye Galleon Press, 1986.

———. *My Journal*. Fairfield, Wash.: Ye Galleon Press, 1982.

"Widely Known Pioneer Is Called to Her Final Rest." *The Post-Intelligencer*, 29 June 1919.

KITTY C. WILKINS

Beal, Merrill D., Ph.D. and Merle W. Wells, Ph.D. *History of Idaho*. Vol. II. New York: Lewis Historical Publishing Company, Inc., 1959.

"Death Takes Colorful Pioneer Horsewoman." *The Idaho Statesman*, 11 October 1936.

Farner, Tom. "The Queen of Diamonds." *Western Horseman*, September (1992): 26–33.

Hart, Arthur A. "Idaho Yesterdays: Horse Queen of Idaho Reaped Much Publicity." *The Idaho Statesman*, 18 December 1972.

"Horses Are Her Delight." *Sioux City Journal*, 26 June 1891.

"Horse Queen of the West." *St. Louis Post-Dispatch*, 10 October 1895.

"Kitty Wilkins 'Horse Queen' Dies Suddenly." *The Idaho Statesman*, 9 October 1936

"Kitty Wilkins Tells Story of Lost Gold Mine Near Jarbidge." *The Idaho Statesman*, 10 January 1926.

"Parents of Idaho's Horse Queen Came West in 1853." *The Idaho Statesman*, 22 April 1928.

"Pioneer Stockman Called By Death." *The Idaho Statesman*, 24 September 1936.

St. John, Harvey. "The Golden Queen." *True West*, July–August (1964): 34–35, 64.

"Their Parents Visit Old Fort Boise in '53." *The Idaho Statesman*, 9 September 1934.

"Twenty Years Ago: The 'Horse Queen of Idaho.'" *The Idaho Statesman*, 18 December 1927.

EMMA RUSSELL YEARIAN

Accola, John. "Grandson of Idaho's 'Sheep Queen' Bases Novel on His Family History." *The Idaho Statesman*, 13 November 1977.

Defenbach, Byron. *IDAHO The Place and Its People*. Chicago–New York: The American Historical Society, Inc., 1933.

"Mrs. Yearian, Idaho Wool Grower, Dies." *The Idaho Daily Statesman*, 26 December 1951.

Penson, Betty. "Emma Russell Yearian's Climb to Fame." *The Idaho Statesman*, 22 January 1978.

———. "The Story of Idaho's Amazing Sheep Queen." *The Idaho Statesman*, 29 January 1978.

Penson-Ward, Betty. *Idaho Women In History*. Boise, Ida.: Legendary Publishing Company, 1991.

Savage, Thomas. *I Heard My Sister Speak My Name*. Boston: Little, Brown and Company, 1977.

Swank, Gladys R. *Ladies of the House (and Senate) History of Idaho Women Legislators Since Statehood*. Lewiston, Ida.: private publisher, 1978.

INDEX